Implementing and Assessing Use-Driven Acquisitions

PRACTICAL GUIDES FOR LIBRARIANS

About the Series

This innovative series written and edited for librarians by librarians provides authoritative, practical information and guidance on a wide spectrum of library processes and operations.

Books in the series are focused, describing practical and innovative solutions to a problem facing today's librarian and delivering step-by-step guidance for planning, creating, implementing, managing, and evaluating a wide range of services and programs.

The books are aimed at beginning and intermediate librarians needing basic instruction/guidance in a specific subject and at experienced librarians who need to gain knowledge in a new area or guidance in implementing a new program/service.

About the Series Editor

The **Practical Guides for Librarians** series was conceived by and is edited by M. Sandra Wood, MLS, MBA, AHIP, FMLA, Librarian Emerita, Penn State University Libraries.

M. Sandra Wood was a librarian at the George T. Harrell Library, The Milton S. Hershey Medical Center, College of Medicine, Pennsylvania State University, Hershey, PA, for over 35 years, specializing in reference, educational, and database services. Ms. Wood worked for several years as a Development Editor for Neal-Schuman Publishers.

Ms. Wood received a MLS from Indiana University and a MBA from the University of Maryland. She is a Fellow of the Medical Library Association and served as a member of MLA's Board of Directors from 1991 to 1995. Ms. Wood is founding and current editor of *Medical Reference Services Quarterly*, now in its 35th volume. She also was founding editor of the *Journal of Consumer Health on the Internet* and the *Journal of Electronic Resources in Medical Libraries* and served as editor/co-editor of both journals through 2011.

Titles in the Series

1. *How to Teach: A Practical Guide for Librarians* by Beverley E. Crane
2. *Implementing an Inclusive Staffing Model for Today's Reference Services* by Julia K. Nims, Paula Storm, and Robert Stevens
3. *Managing Digital Audiovisual Resources: A Practical Guide for Librarians* by Matthew C. Mariner
4. *Outsourcing Technology: A Practical Guide for Librarians* by Robin Hastings
5. *Making the Library Accessible for All: A Practical Guide for Librarians* by Jane Vincent

6. *Discovering and Using Historical Geographical Resources on the Web: A Practical Guide for Librarians* by Eva H. Dodsworth and L. W. Laliberté
7. *Digitization and Digital Archiving: A Practical Guide for Librarians* by Elizabeth R. Leggett
8. *Makerspaces: A Practical Guide for Librarians* by John J. Burke
9. *Implementing Web-Scale Discovery Services: A Practical Guide for Librarians* by JoLinda Thompson
10. *Using iPhones and iPads: A Practical Guide for Librarians* by Matthew Connolly and Tony Cosgrave
11. *Usability Testing: A Practical Guide for Librarians* by Rebecca Blakiston
12. *Mobile Devices: A Practical Guide for Librarians* by Ben Rawlins
13. *Going Beyond Loaning Books to Loaning Technologies: A Practical Guide for Librarians* by Janelle Sander, Lori S. Mestre, and Eric Kurt
14. *Children's Services Today: A Practical Guide for Librarians* by Jeanette Larson
15. *Genealogy: A Practical Guide for Librarians* by Katherine Pennavaria
16. *Collection Evaluation in Academic Libraries: A Practical Guide for Librarians* by Karen C. Kohn
17. *Creating Online Tutorials: A Practical Guide for Librarians* by Hannah Gascho Rempel and Maribeth Slebodnik
18. *Using Google Earth in Libraries: A Practical Guide for Librarians* by Eva Dodsworth and Andrew Nicholson
19. *Integrating the Web into Everyday Library Services: A Practical Guide for Librarians* by Elizabeth R. Leggett
20. *Infographics: A Practical Guide for Librarians* by Beverley E. Crane
21. *Meeting Community Needs: A Practical Guide for Librarians* by Pamela H. MacKellar
22. *3D Printing: A Practical Guide for Librarians* by Sara Russell Gonzalez and Denise Beaubien Bennett
23. *Implementing and Assessing Use-Driven Acquisitions: A Practical Guide for Librarians* by Steven Carrico, Michelle Leonard, and Erin Gallagher

Implementing and Assessing Use-Driven Acquisitions

A Practical Guide for Librarians

Steven Carrico
Michelle Leonard
Erin Gallagher

with contributions from
Trey Shelton

PRACTICAL GUIDES FOR LIBRARIANS, NO. 23

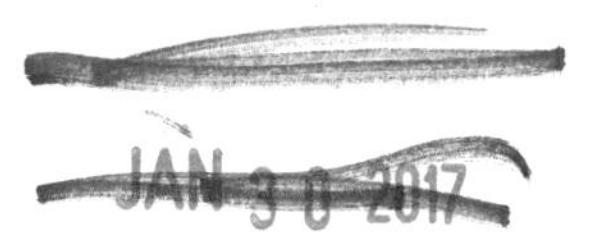

ROWMAN & LITTLEFIELD
Lanham • Boulder • New York • London

Published by Rowman & Littlefield
A wholly owned subsidiary of The Rowman & Littlefield Publishing Group, Inc.
4501 Forbes Boulevard, Suite 200, Lanham, Maryland 20706
www.rowman.com

Unit A, Whitacre Mews, 26-34 Stannary Street, London SE11 4AB

British Library Cataloguing in Publication Information Available

Library of Congress Cataloging-in-Publication Data

Names: Carrico, Steve, author. | Leonard, Michelle, 1968–, author. | Gallagher, Erin, 1982–, author. | Shelton, Trey, contributor.
Title: Implementing and assessing use-driven acquisitions : a practical guide for librarians / Steven Carrico, Michelle Leonard, Erin Gallagher ; with contributions from Trey Shelton.
Description: Lanham : Rowman & Littlefield, [2016] | Series: Practical guides for librarians ; 23 | Includes bibliographical references and index.
Identifiers: LCCN 2015038768| ISBN 9781442262751 (hardcover : alk. paper) | ISBN 9781442262768 (pbk. : alk. paper) | ISBN 9781442262775 (ebook)
Subjects: LCSH: Use-driven acquisitions (Libraries)
Classification: LCC Z689 .C287 2016 | DDC 025.2—dc23 LC record available at http://lccn.loc.gov/2015038768

∞™ The paper used in this publication meets the minimum requirements of American National Standard for Information Sciences—Permanence of Paper for Printed Library Materials, ANSI/NISO Z39.48-1992.

Printed in the United States of America

Contents

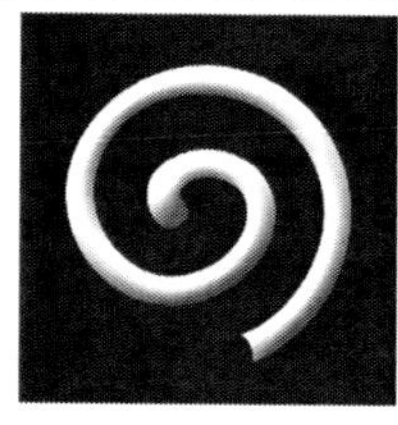

List of Illustrations ix

List of Library Case Studies and Vendor Spotlights xi

Preface xiii

Part 1: Developing Use-Driven Acquisition Plans

Chapter 1 **Use-Driven Acquisition Project Management** 3

Chapter 2 **Collections and Budget Strategies** 13

Chapter 3 **Working with Vendors and Content Providers** 25

Part 2: E-Book UDA Plans

Chapter 4 **Demand-Driven Acquisitions (DDA)** 39

Chapter 5 **Evidence-Based Acquisitions (EBA)** 58

Chapter 6 **Shared and Consortia Plans** 70

Part 3: Targeting Libraries and Collections

Chapter 7 **Patron-Driven Acquisition of Print Materials, by Trey Shelton** 85

Chapter 8 **Interlibrary Loan—Purchase on Demand (PoD)** 95

Chapter 9 **Streaming Video, by Trey Shelton** 108

Chapter 10 **Patron-Driven Acquisition in Public and Special Libraries** 122

Part 4: Evaluation and Emerging Strategies

Chapter 11 **Assessment of UDA Plans** 131

Chapter 12 **Future Directions** 142

Appendix 1. UDA Library Survey 148

Appendix 2. PDA Public Library Survey 152

Glossary 155

Index 157

About the Authors and Contributor 159

List of Illustrations

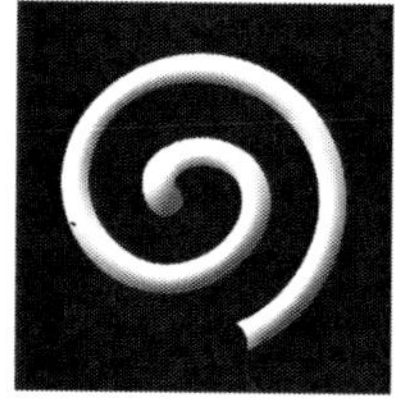

Figures

Figure P.1. Use-driven acquisition models xiv

Figure 4.1. Project planning sequence 50

Figure 7.1. Print PDA item display in catalog 89

Figure 7.2. Print PDA item request form 89

Figure 9.1. Example of a streaming-video usage report 113

Figure 10.1. Example of a public library catalog record with RTL 124

Tables

Table 1.1. Checklist for implementing a UDA program 7

Table 3.1. List of vendors 28

Table 3.2. Library/vendor responsibilities 32

Table 4.1. E-book UDA selection models 40

Table 4.2. E-book DDA licensing models 41

Table 4.3. Profile prep checklist 44

Table 5.1. List of EBA content providers 60

Table 8.1. Checklist for implementing a PoD program 98

Table 9.1. Streaming-video UDA models 110

Table 9.2. Example of a library-generated cost-per-use report 115

Table 11.1. UDA Library Survey, question 11: "How is the PDA/DDA program evaluated?" 133

Table 11.2. UDA Library Survey, question 12: "How often is your PDA/DDA program evaluated?" 133

Table 11.3. Snapshot of a publisher-supplied cost-usage report for an EBA plan 135

Table 11.4. Example of a vendor-library cost-usage report for purchased e-books—DDA 135

Table 11.5. Example of a library-generated cost-use STL report 137

Table 11.6. Example of a library-generated cost-usage report for DDA (2009–2012) 138

List of Library Case Studies and Vendor Spotlights

Library Case Studies

Chapter 1: Memorial University Libraries (Newfoundland) 11

Chapter 2: California State University, Fullerton, Pollak Library 20

Chapter 2: University of Florida Smathers Libraries 22

Chapter 4: Rollins College Library 52

Chapter 4: Nova Southeastern University Libraries 53

Chapter 4: University of North Carolina at Chapel Hill Libraries 55

Chapter 5: Brigham Young University Library 65

Chapter 6: Florida State University Libraries 79

Chapter 7: University of Arizona Library 91

Chapter 7: Drake University Library 93

Chapter 8: University of Chicago Library 104

Chapter 8: The Ohio State University Libraries 105

Chapter 8: University of Nebraska, Lincoln Libraries 106

Chapter 9: University of North Carolina at Greensboro Libraries 116

Vendor Spotlights

Chapter 3: ProQuest Coutts 33

Chapter 3: YBP Library Services 35

Chapter 5: Wiley 68

Chapter 9: Kanopy Streaming Video 118

Chapter 9: Alexander Street Press 120

Preface

The emergence of use-driven acquisition (UDA) signifies a recent but powerful shift in how libraries acquire materials and online resources. UDA models, such as demand-driven acquisition and evidence-based acquisition, are sparking enormous changes in collection development practices for academic and public libraries. Several factors explain the rise of use-driven acquisition: the growing propensity for online resources; the trend for many academic libraries to reduce traditional book acquisitions and downscale print collections; and costs incurred being based on usage (to incorporate UDA as an innovative means to enhance the cost-benefit of library budgets).

Another factor for the growth of UDA plans in libraries is the pragmatic merging of *just-in-time* with *just-in-case* approaches to collection building. For decades, academic libraries focused on acquiring vast book and journal holdings with the intent to build collections for the ages. Libraries had larger budgets, more staff, and ample space to build large collections *just in case* the items were used one day. Libraries now face restrictive budgets, downsizing, and less shelving space. In an online environment, with technology that supports the application of UDA plans, libraries can offer books and other resources using a just-in-time approach. Although libraries are getting creative in finding a balance between the two collection philosophies, use-driven acquisition plans are having a significant effect on the relationship between libraries, vendors, and publishers.

We bring unique perspectives to this book since we are acquisitions, e-resources, and collection management librarians who have extensive experience working with UDA plans in academic libraries as well as a leading book vendor. *Implementing and Assessing Use-Driven Acquisitions: A Practical Guide for Librarians* is designed to assist library professionals as they partner with vendors and publishers to implement and manage use-driven acquisition plans. The book reviews the various models of UDA being employed in libraries and offers methods for assessing various aspects of UDA plans. In addition to the practical side, the theoretical applications of use-driven acquisition plans and how they affect collection building and budgeting are highlighted, both for individual libraries and library consortia.

For the purposes of this book, *use-driven acquisitions* is the overarching term that incorporates multiple models and applies to any method of collection development in which content is acquired based on patron discovery and use rather than the anticipation of patron use. UDA includes demand-driven acquisition (DDA), also referred to as pa-

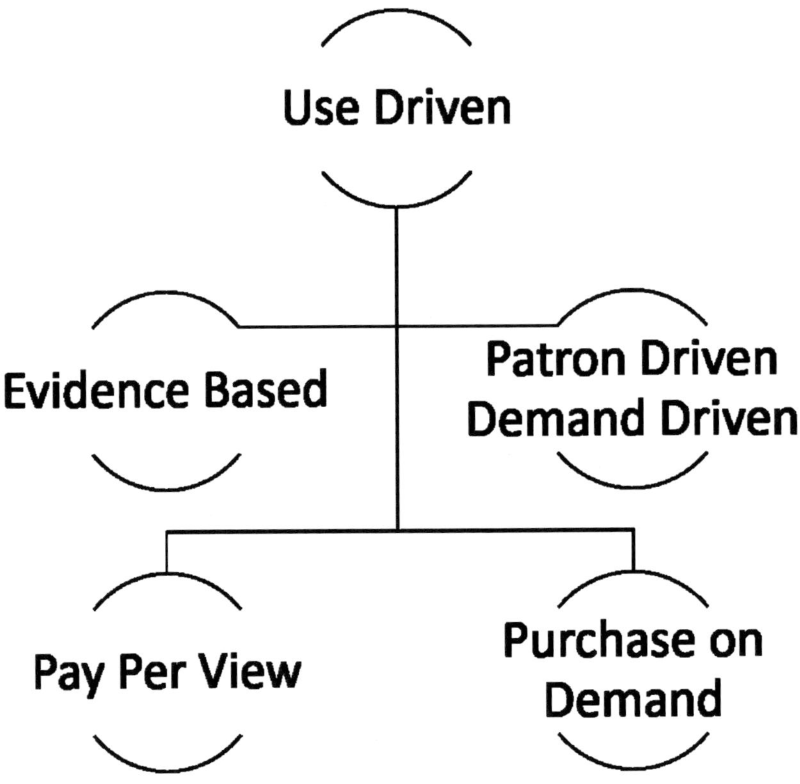

Figure P.1. Use-driven acquisition models

tron-driven acquisition (PDA), and evidence-based acquisition (EBA). These two models are the most recognized and prevalent in libraries, but two other models also fit under the UDA umbrella: purchase on demand (PoD) and pay per view (PPV), as shown in figure P.1. We contend that use-driven acquisition models are valuable tools for collection building, and libraries will continue to incorporate these models into their acquisitions and budget strategies in the coming years.

Organization

This book is divided into four sections. Part 1, "Developing Use-Driven Acquisition Plans," contains chapters 1 through 3. Chapter 1, "Use-Driven Acquisition Project Management," describes the basic elements and features of each use-driven acquisition model, recommends using project management fundamentals, and demonstrates the benefits of running a pilot program. Chapter 2, "Collections and Budget Strategies," details how use-driven acquisition plans can be integrated into collection development. Chapter 3, "Working with Vendors and Content Providers," focuses on forging beneficial library partnerships with vendors and publishers in the implementation of UDA plans.

Part 2, "E-Book UDA Plans," contains chapters 4 through 6. Chapter 4, "Demand-Driven Acquisitions (DDA)," is a "how-to" primer for libraries on developing and managing DDA plans that acquire e-books. Chapter 5, "Evidence-Based Acquisitions (EBA)," concentrates on a model that is growing in popularity. Chapter 6, "Shared and Consortia Plans," details the challenges and benefits of launching multilibrary UDA plans.

Part 3, "Targeting Libraries and Collections," contains chapters 7 through 10. Chapter 7, "Patron-Driven Acquisition of Print Materials," written by Trey Shelton, explains how PDA plans are used to acquire print monographs and other materials such as music scores. Chapter 8, "Interlibrary Loan—Purchase on Demand (PoD)," offers the basic design and recommendations to manage a model from an ILL Department. Chapter 9, "Streaming Video," also written by Trey Shelton, provides a summary of options for implementing a UDA plan to acquire access to online videos. Chapter 10, "Patron-Driven Acquisition in Public and Special Libraries," summarizes how UDA is applied in nonacademic library environments.

Part 4, "Evaluation and Emerging Strategies," contains the final two chapters in the book. Chapter 11, "Assessment of UDA Plans," explains the value of assessing a UDA plan to determine cost-effectiveness, provide evidence in making modifications, and share results with stakeholders. Chapter 12, "Future Directions," is an essay on how we envision the future of UDA plans that also contains recommendations for publishers, vendors, and librarians.

Many chapters in *Implementing and Assessing Use-Driven Acquisitions* offer case studies and vendor spotlights (located at the end of the chapters) and refer to them within the text to provide real-world examples of how libraries and content providers are approaching UDA. Case studies are summarized interviews with librarians who share valuable experience in deploying UDA models in their libraries. Vendor spotlights are condensed discussions we held with vendor and publisher representatives who offer insightful commentary from a business perspective. Cited books, articles, blog posts, websites, and assorted publications are included as references, as well as numerous checklists that can aid in planning and project management. Important terms are found in the glossary.

Implementing and Assessing Use-Driven Acquisitions: A Practical Guide for Librarians also has two appendixes containing the questions from the original surveys we conducted. Appendix 1, "UDA Library Survey," comprising nineteen questions, was distributed to several academic library listservs in late 2014 with approximately 515 responses from librarians, administrators, and staff working in a variety of libraries—mostly academic. The "UDA Library Survey" includes many interesting free-text responses on various facets of use-driven acquisition plans ongoing in libraries. Appendix 2 contains the "PDA Public Library Survey," which comprises twelve questions and was distributed only to public library listservs in mid-2015 with sixty-four responses. Each appendix provides a link to the University of Florida George A. Smathers Libraries' institutional repository, which contains the complete survey questions and responses. Readers are welcome to use and cite the surveys.

We are confident that use-driven acquisitions will become ubiquitous in libraries and be an ongoing element of collection development management strategies. There are many options for libraries to consider, and UDA models, products, and services are evolving quickly. *Implementing and Assessing Use-Driven Acquisitions* is a reference for libraries of all types and will empower library professionals in making informed decisions on which UDA model or models work best for their unique settings.

Part 1

DEVELOPING USE-DRIVEN ACQUISITION PLANS

CHAPTER 1

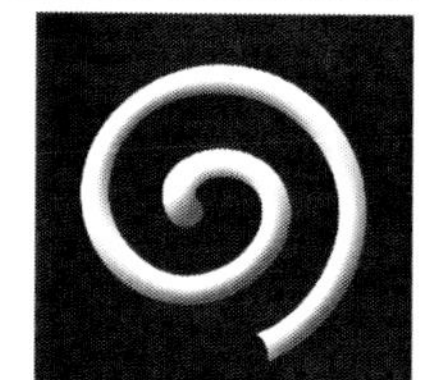

Use-Driven Acquisition Project Management

IN THIS CHAPTER

- ▷ Reviewing the UDA models
- ▷ Asking the right questions: do your research
- ▷ Using project management: following checklists for project organization
- ▷ Describing the value of a pilot program

A LARGE COMPONENT OF TRADITIONAL collection management in libraries is designed for librarians to select books and other materials. The process involves many departments and begins with the librarian who selects books and other materials for purchase, the acquisitions staff that places the order, catalogers who create records in the catalog, and the patrons who view the purchased materials. With the advent of use-driven acquisition (UDA) plans, the purchases are based on patron recommendations or by the number of times the material is used or viewed by the patron. Currently, the trend in collection building is a blend of librarian selection and patron requests or a method driven by usage. This chapter will describe the different types of UDA models and offer methods of applying project management tools, such as a simplified checklist, to use when tracking the steps of the UDA plan implementation. The value of use-driven acquisitions and running pilot programs is highlighted, and a library case study concludes the chapter.

Overview of Use-Driven Acquisition Models

Most of the literature on collection-building strategies focuses on case studies in one library or in a consortium. This type of practical experience provides the reader with the challenges and successes of how use-driven models function in a particular library setting. The four models of use-driven acquisition most widely implemented in all types of libraries are defined below.

Definitions

Patron-Driven Acquisition (PDA) / Demand-Driven Acquisition (DDA). PDA/DDA is the most common UDA model and is a partnership between the library and an aggregator and/or book vendor, as the plan offers the acquisition of print or e-books, or a combination of both. With this plan, profiles and parameters are built (similar to an approval plan) and corresponding MARC records are loaded into the library catalog where access and purchases are derived directly from use.

Evidence-Based Acquisition (EBA). With the EBA model, a library deposits funds with a publisher. The publisher then provides their own content—usually e-books. A set number of MARC records are loaded into the library catalog or activated through the discovery service. At the end of a specific time frame, purchases are made using the deposit funds based on e-book usage or library selection.

Interlibrary Loan Purchase on Demand (ILL-PoD). The ILL-PoD model is the original UDA model. In this example, patrons submit a request for material not owned by the library to their interlibrary loan department. The ILL requests that meet established criteria for print, e-books, or other formats are purchased and then loaned to patrons. In most cases, the books and materials purchased from a PoD plan are eventually cataloged and placed into library collections.

Pay per View (PPV). PPV is a model that allows libraries a method of offering users access to journal articles on demand. Libraries pay publishers (sometimes via vendor agents) to provide their users with full access to journal articles from unsubscribed journals.

The Basic Components

All UDA plans have one major characteristic—usage drives acquisitions—but vary in design, format, and workflow to some degree. There are standard models that can be tailored to meet a library's specific collections and budget. All UDA models offer some level of customization for any library, but this may vary by vendor or publisher. One popular model, for example, is the DDA e-book plan that is offered by aggregators, because they partner with multiple publishers to provide a variety of content. Offering content from multiple publishers, however, may complicate a UDA plan because each publisher has their own restrictions for use, including multiple- versus single-user access, chapter downloads, and print-per-page limitations.

Questions to Address

Prior to launching UDA, libraries should research the current literature, reach out to colleagues who are currently conducting UDA programs, and hold conversations with vendors on the type of UDA model offered to determine the best plan for their library. Before launching a UDA plan, there are many questions to address, including the following:

- What is the length of the plan? Should there be a pilot, a predetermined period with a defined end date, or an ongoing program?
- Is the focus of the model on access or ownership? Or both?
- For the DDA plan, who are the best publishers to include, or exclude?
- For an EBA plan, which publishers are available, what is the cost, and what content do they offer?
- What is the scope and content of the plan? Parameters include readership level, imprint years, subject areas, language, and format.
- What is the budget?
- What are the technical specifications of the plan and workflow?
- What technical support is required (i.e., record loading and holdings uploads)?
- How will reports based on cost of the material and/or usage be generated? What reports can the vendor/aggregator provide?
- How will the library and vendor/aggregator coordinate when dealing with unexpected challenges (i.e., budget, content selection) of the UDA plan?

Project Management: Use of Checklists to Organize the Project

With the intricacies and coordination of a UDA plan, keeping track of the workflow is crucial. Therefore, libraries should develop project management protocols, or at the very least follow a detailed task management chart. Libraries may have a subscription to project management software (e.g., Microsoft Project) or may use one of the free products (e.g., Trello). If implanting project management software is not an option, it is easy to create your own project management plans using Microsoft Excel or Word. The next page illustrates a time line including project phases, key players, and key activities that are crucial for organizational purposes and planning. This project management time line is modified from a Gantt chart and created in Word. A time line with phases and responsibilities is helpful when implementing a UDA plan and can serve as a reference when demonstrating the UDA workflow to library administrators or staff.

Libraries should also utilize a checklist to track the implementation of a UDA plan. Table 1.1 shows a simple checklist created in an Excel spreadsheet. The checklist includes five phases and multiple steps within each phase. The phases are as follows: (1) set goals and objectives; (2) devise workflow; (3) define parameters; (4) launch plan; and (5) review and assessment. Dividing the implementation into large phases with multiple steps allows a library to keep the project organized. The "Checklist for Implementing a UDA Program" identifies the sequential order of the steps.

Phase 1: Set Goals and Objectives

Developing clear and attainable goals for a use-driven acquisition plan is paramount to any successful program. The objectives should be tied to the goals. In this phase, you will identify collections that will be included. The amount of funding and whether it is one-time or recurring dictates the scale and length of a plan. One-time funding to initiate a pilot or nonrecurring plan is a viable option, but developing a sustainable budget to run an ongoing plan will be less work and distress in the long term. The expansion or reduction of a plan usually revolves around the budget and rate of spend. If UDA funds are being expended too quickly, you should consider narrowing the parameters of the plan; in

PROJECT PLANNING: TIMELINE AND PHASES OF IMPLEMENTATION

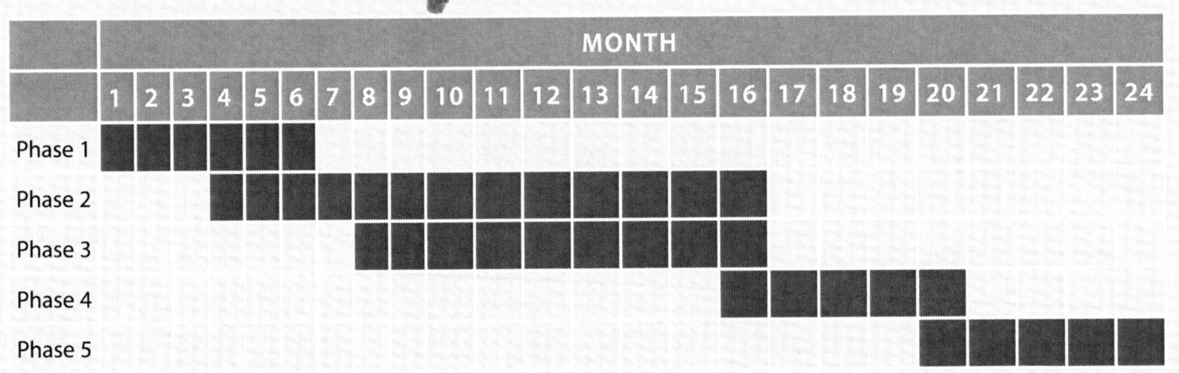

Phase 1. Name of Phase

- Time frame:
- Key personnel:
- Key activities:

Phase 2. Name of Phase

- Time frame:
- Key personnel:
- Key activities:

Phase 3. Name of Phase

- Time frame:
- Key personnel:
- Key activities:

Phase 4. Name of Phase

- Time frame:
- Key personnel:
- Key activities:

Phase 5. Name of Phase

- Time frame:
- Key personnel:
- Key activities:

Table 1.1. Checklist for implementing a UDA program

PHASE	STEPS	CHECK AS YOU GO
Phase 1: Set goals & objectives	1. Identify collections and user needs	☐
	2. Set collection strategies	☐
	3. Identify budget options and amount	☐
	4. Choose UDA model	☐
Phase 2: Devise workflow	1. Coordinate with other acquisition streams	☐
	2. Create a budget plan	☐
	3. Establish staff responsibilities	☐
	4. Define reports and customer support	☐
	5. Determine delivery methods to users	☐
Phase 3: Define parameters	1. Meet with subject specialists	☐
	2. Select types of materials, language, etc.	☐
	3. Determine users (e.g., faculty, grad student, etc.)	☐
	4. Review back-file content	☐
Phase 4: Launch plan	1. Set an implementation date	☐
	2. Set schedule of usage review and title selection	☐
	3. Establish deposit account and invoices	☐
	4. Load MARC e-book records into catalog	☐
Phase 5: Review & assessment	1. Determine the reports to generate	☐
	2. Check workflow and technical aspects	☐
	3. Track expenditures and usage	☐
	4. Conduct user studies or surveys	☐

the reverse, if funds are not being spent, you should consider expanding the parameters. Once the parameters are determined, and the budget set, the review of various UDA models begins. There are several models, so a list of pros and cons for each model should be developed so you can chose the models that best serve your needs.

Phase 2: Devise Workflow

Librarians implementing UDA plans should consider which departments and staff members should be involved and during which stages. Smaller libraries that only have one or two staff members may prefer to implement a simple UDA plan, perhaps a single-type format or discipline. This program should streamline workflow and benefit library users. UDA plans will involve processes and tasks that must be incorporated into existing workflows. Acquisition streams indicate the "traditional" streams of acquisitions, meaning approval plans, firm ordering, package e-book purchases, and so forth. From budgeting to acquisitions, and from collection development to record loading and maintenance, it is necessary to designate staff to handle key operations. Regardless of the level of funding a library has to support UDA plans, it is crucial to evaluate the plan often to ensure you stay within your budget. Most content providers will notify libraries when they approach their deposit limit, but expenditures should be monitored throughout the course of the plan as well. You should evaluate the content being loaned or purchased to determine which subject areas are responsible for the bulk of usage; the results may warrant a change in how funds are allocated. The larger the library's budget, the more ambitious the plan can be.

For example, a well-funded DDA e-book plan should include broader parameters such as older publication years, higher price caps per title for purchase or short-term loans, or more inclusive subject areas.

Phase 3: Define Parameters

Targeting collections of specific subject areas is a key element of any UDA plan. All UDA models involve some type of profile development in which subject and nonsubject parameters are determined. These parameters act as the filtering system through which only titles that fit the library's criteria are made available for patron discovery and use. Profiles should be built to accommodate goals of the plan and to fulfill the needs of library users, whether academic, specialized, or public. Selecting the format and model of UDA plan are important first steps because the library must have infrastructure in place (e.g., streaming). While the majority of use-driven acquisition plans in academic libraries focus on e-books, other formats are emerging in the UDA landscape, including streaming video, journal articles, online dissertations, music, and musical scores, to name just a few. Reviewing back files or vendor content is the first step in the evaluation of a UDA plan. This is the step where libraries need to ensure content is acceptable.

Phase 4: Launch Plan

Setting an exact date for the launch of a new UDA plan is problematic due to many factors and steps involved in the implementation. These time frames can usually be negotiated between the library and vendor or publisher, and agreed upon a few months in advance. For example, a library may wish to start a UDA plan in the summer during the break between the busier fall and spring semesters. Implementation dates may also coincide with library budget cycles; libraries running UDA plans with deposit accounts may have strict rules regarding fiscal year allocation and expenditures and should create a time line for the plan accordingly.

Once setup is finished, if the plan is a DDA or other plan acquiring e-books, the MARC records are loaded into a library catalog or discovery service to become the consideration or discovery pool. The records immediately become visible and accessible to users who are usually unaware the e-books are part of a use-driven model. Access to online materials is relatively instantaneous, and some libraries add an online message that markets the service.

Phase 5: Review and Assessment

Ongoing evaluation, management, and modification of the plan are required for sustainability. Assessment provides the evidence needed to make adjustments to workflows and profiles, both of which are crucial to maintaining successful UDA plans. A key element of assessment is sharing the results of the plan, including cost and usage incurred, with stakeholders and those who are in positions to influence ongoing support. For more on evaluating and modifying UDA plans, refer to chapter 11, "Assessment of UDA Plans."

The Value of a Pilot Program

A pilot is a short-term (time-limited) program that serves as a test case for determining if a UDA model is both beneficial and affordable. For libraries new to use-driven acquisitions, it is recommended to start small with a pilot program because UDA plans require modifications to and maintenance of the plan after implementation. Pilot programs provide hard data on cost and usage that can be used to tweak parameters and develop a more robust UDA program moving forward. If a pilot program is successful, results can provide positive interactions with collection managers. For special or public libraries, positive results from pilot projects can be helpful in swaying administrators or fiscal officers that acquiring resources based on usage can be a cost-effective use of funds. Vendors and publishers can be extraordinarily knowledgeable about the types of plans they offer and can share experiences working with libraries in designing UDA plans, but a pilot program imparts an experimental cushion for a library before committing long term to a UDA method.

Most UDA pilot programs run for a year or less, with the time frame based on the library's budget. For example, after three months, a library should run reports based on actual usage, budget, and scope of content to determine if the plan needs to be modified. Because a pilot is temporary, alterations can be made quickly. Librarians should be careful to note the length of the pilot and the time of the year during which it was run: did it run during the semester at the height of library use, or in the summer when usage tends to be lower? At the end of the pilot, the library should review final cost-usage statistics and solicit feedback from selectors, administrators, and acquisitions staff as to the success of the plan based on the original goals.

Many libraries that began with pilot UDA programs are now funding them annually. One patron-driven pilot that is relatively uncomplicated to implement and operate is through the interlibrary loan department (see chapter 8, "Interlibrary Loan—Purchase on Demand [PoD]"). Another is a use-driven pilot in which an existing approval or slip plan is used as the launch pad for determining the content in your discovery pool. This option is usually operated under the guidance of the acquisitions and/or e-resources department.

Key Points

Although libraries partner with vendors and publishers to implement and manage UDA plans, it is prudent for libraries to take an active role in the process. Using project management applications assists with the organization of each plan. Running a pilot UDA program can be extremely helpful for libraries that are new to the UDA plan where adjustments are easily made, prior to full implementation of a plan. Here are the main points to remember going forward:

- There are four major models of UDA to meet a library's specific needs and goals: patron-driven acquisitions (PDA); evidence-based acquisitions (EBA); interlibrary loan purchase on demand (PoD); and pay per view (PPV).
- Libraries should use a series of questions to determine key information to assist them in working with vendors and publishers to design a UDA plan.

- Utilizing project management tools such as a simplified checklist can provide a basic guide to building and managing a successful program.
- Pilot programs are a great way to introduce UDA programs. A pilot allows vendors, publishers, and library staff time to assess and make adjustments to workflow, budget, and collection profiles including parameters and supplied content.

In the next chapter, the focus will shift to the important issues of collection building and material budgeting, and how libraries can revise strategies to incorporate UDA plans.

Further Reading

"ALA Applauds Macmillan's Ebook Pilot for Libraries." 2013. *American Libraries* 44, no. 3: 7.

Anderson, Elsa K. 2014. "Workflow Analysis." *Library Technology Reports* 50, no. 3: 23–29.

Beisler, Amalia, and Lisa Kurt. 2012. "E-Book Workflow from Inquiry to Access: Facing the Challenges to Implementing E-Book Access at the University of Nevada, Reno." *Collaborative Librarianship* 4, no. 3: 96–116.

"Biz Acq Workflows in Paradise: EBooks, Acquisitions, and Cataloging." 2010. *Against the Grain* 22, no. 4: 56–59.

Bunnelle, James. 2012. "Pilot to Program: Demand-Driven E-Books at the Orbis-Cascade Consortium, 1 Year Later." *Against the Grain* 24, no. 5: 24–28.

De Fino, Melissa, and Mei Ling Lo. 2011. "New Roads for Patron-Driven E-Books: Collection Development and Technical Services Implications of a Patron-Driven Acquisitions Pilot at Rutgers." *Journal of Electronic Resources Librarianship* 23, no. 4: 327–38. doi:10.1080/1941126x.2011.627043.

Downey, Kay. 2014. "Technical Services Workflow for Book Jobber-Mediated Demand Driven E-book Acquisitions." *Technical Services Quarterly* 31, no. 1: 1–12. doi:10.1080/07317131.2014.844617.

Emery, Jill, and Bonnie Parks. 2012. "The Demand Driven Acquisitions Pilot Project by the Orbis Cascade Alliance: An Interview with Members of the Demand Driven Acquisitions Implementation Team." *Serials Review* 38, no. 2 (June): 132–36. doi:10.1016/j.serrev.2012.04.008.

Herrera, Gail, and Judy Greenwood. 2011. "Patron-Initiated Purchasing: Evaluating Criteria and Workflows." *Journal of Interlibrary Loan, Document Delivery and Electronic Reserves* 21, nos. 1–2: 9–24. doi:10.1080/1072303X.2011.544602.

Hoppe, Elizabeth, and Courtney Seymour. 2012. "Going Above and Beyond: Building an Interdisciplinary Undergraduate Research Collection via an ILL POD Program." *Against the Grain* 24, no. 4: 26–34.

Mackinder, Lisa. 2014. "The Seemingly Endless Challenge: Workflows." *Serials Librarian* 67, no. 2: 158–65. doi:10.1080/0361526X.2014.940481.

Maddox Abbott, Jennifer A., and Mary S. Laskowski. 2014. "So Many Projects, So Few Resources: Using Effective Project Management in Technical Services." *Collection Management* 39, no. 2: 161–76. doi:10.1080/01462679.2014.891492.

Morris, Jill. 2015. "Home Grown Ebooks: North Carolina's Collaborative Ebook Pilot Project." *Collaborative Librarianship* 7, no. 1: 16–21.

Thomas, Joseph, Heather Racine, and Dan Shouse. 2013. "EBooks and Efficiencies in Acquisitions Expenditures and Workflows." *Against the Grain* 25, no. 2: 14–18.

Library Case Study: Memorial University Libraries (Newfoundland)

Reporting: Diane Keeping, collection development librarian

Faculty: ~1,400 academic staff members; **Students:** ~15,000 full-time enrollment (FTE)

Type of institution: public

Memberships/consortia: Canadian Association of Research Libraries (CARL); Council of Atlantic University Libraries (CAUL); Canadian Research Knowledge Network (CRKN); Council of Prairie and Pacific University Libraries (COPPUL)—affiliate membership.

Colleges/programs/research centers supported: The libraries support several campuses, including the main St. John's Campus, Grenfell Campus, Marine Institute, Health Sciences, Harlow, and the Labrador Institute. The libraries support several certificate, diploma, and bachelor's, master's, and doctoral degree programs in a variety of subjects.

Materials budget: fiscal year (FY) 2015: $8,000,000 (approx.)

Number of use-driven acquisition (PDA/DDA) plans: One e-book DDA pilot plan with Yankee Book Peddler (YBP) and one print-format "collection development on demand" program in the main branch, which involves purchasing instead of borrowing books that are requested through interlibrary loan if they meet the libraries' established criteria for purchase.

Features of the pilot plan: The libraries use a combination of aggregators in the DDA program to maximize the amount of content available to users. YBP is the libraries' main monograph vendor and coordinates existing acquisition streams with the DDA program. YBP allows the libraries to use multiple e-book aggregators without duplicating content. The libraries also take advantage of YBP's profiling features so the DDA plan complements existing slip-approval plans and offers content appropriate. YBP's GOBI (collections) database indicates which titles are included in the DDA plan, and this is a useful tool for librarians when they are making their selection decisions. The DDA plan includes all general academic and professional content-level e-book publications within the Library of Congress ranges that are covered in the slip-approval plan.

Budget of the UDA plan: There is no set budget allocation, but approximately 10 percent of the monograph budget has been tentatively earmarked. The pilot with YBP is intended to provide data to determine an appropriate allocation for an e-book DDA program, if the libraries decide to implement DDA as a standard process.

Goals and reasons for incorporating UDA: The goal of the pilot DDA was to provide immediate access to a greater number of e-books within the confines of the existing monographs budget. Implemented as a signature project of the libraries' larger strategic planning, it was hoped the pilot would decrease the reliance on anticipatory purchasing and increase frequency with which patrons have immediate access to materials of interest.

Workflow and maintenance: The libraries addressed technical glitches and workflow issues as they arose. The libraries receive and delete files from our main e-book aggregator.

Assessment and reporting: Based on the cost/usage data that are available so far, the DDA program has provided access to 1,616 unique titles for an average cost of $21.08. From that perspective, it does appear to be showing a good return on investment. The bulk of the DDA spending, not surprisingly, is on short-term loans (STLs) that amount to a little over three times the amount spent on DDA e-book purchases.

Challenges

- The library is generally satisfied with allowing three STLs. However, a stated concern is the rising prices of STLs; the library will reconsider reducing the number of loans permitted or removing publishers that are charging too much for STLs.
- The library is seeing some duplication of titles in the DDA pool with content included in subscribed or purchased e-book packages. Although series and selected publishers are excluded in the DDA plan, the approach does not always prevent duplication with large multidisciplinary, multipublisher e-book packages.
- Instability in the list price of the DDA e-books and the STL pricing is a serious problem that the library is monitoring closely. Titles with unacceptable price increases are being removed from the consideration pool; some publishers have been excluded from the DDA plan because of the increases in their STL pricing. Again, this level of monitoring is more work for the library, but with a limited budget, the STL price increases are not sustainable.

Branding and marketing: None

Consortia UDA plans: There are no consortia plans.

Success of UDA: Aside from the headaches caused by the need to delete files, the duplication of e-book records in the catalog, and the larger philosophical issues with e-books in general, librarians who are responsible for collections at Memorial Libraries seem to be satisfied with the range of content that is being offered. The DDA profile was designed to represent the interests of four branch libraries and is therefore quite broad in terms of subject coverage and yet focused on academic/professional level publications, so the actual content has been satisfactory and sometimes quite revealing. We've discovered that there is a demand for content in academic areas that are not taught at this university and therefore have not been collection priorities. For example, the university does not offer a veterinary sciences program, but there has been activity on some of the veterinary science books in our DDA pool.

Recommendations for Other Librarians

- Add customizations to the DDA records so they can be identified and pulled out of the library catalog if necessary.
- Don't limit the subject coverage of the DDA plan based on assumptions of which users will or won't be receptive to e-books. Sometimes the results will surprise you.
- If the library already subscribes to a large e-book package, select the vendor of that package as your main DDA e-book supplier. It will help to prevent some of the duplication of e-book titles in your catalog and potential duplicate purchases of the same e-book title on different platforms.
- Monitor your DDA plan closely. Does your content match your profiling parameters? Do your records have all of the customizations that you wanted? Are you being invoiced for the right titles? Have the prices been inflated beyond the price cap initially set for the project? Vendors do make errors. Sometimes the errors can be costly or time consuming to fix.

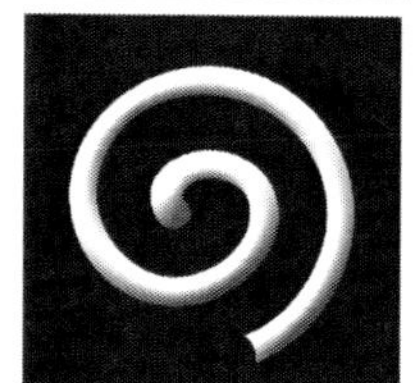

CHAPTER 2

Collections and Budget Strategies

IN THIS CHAPTER

- ▷ Implementing UDA into collection planning
- ▷ Revising collection strategies
- ▷ Incorporating approval plans
- ▷ Budgeting

THIS CHAPTER WILL FOCUS ON THE challenge of incorporating use-driven acquisition (UDA) plans into collection building and budgets in academic libraries. Libraries willing to accommodate increased *just-in-time* practices (immediate purchase) should set clear objectives of how the UDA plan will complement current collection and acquisitions methodologies often rooted in the traditional just-in-case (purchase and hope it is used) philosophy. Suggestions for developing collection and budget strategies to encompass UDA plans are presented, with two academic libraries serving as library case studies.

Collection Planning

Many academic libraries are incorporating use-driven acquisition (UDA) into collection planning. From a series of interviews with vendors in 2012, it was estimated that between four and six hundred institutions were engaged in patron-driven acquisition (PDA) projects (Esposito, 2012). Although far from a scientific study, it does provide librarians with a rough idea of the popularity of use-driven acquisitions. Three years later, the number of libraries administering a UDA program could conceivably be two or three times that guesstimate. In 2015, a representative from one of the prominent e-books aggregators

REASONS TO INCORPORATE UDA WITH TRADITIONAL COLLECTION BUILDING

- ✓ Individual (librarian) selection and approval plans are used to acquire print books that often go unused or under used.
- ✓ Traditional just-in-case collection building is becoming more difficult to justify to library administrators faced with restrictive budgets.
- ✓ Traditional print book purchases require workflow across multiple departments, often including collection management, acquisitions, cataloging, circulation, and stacks maintenance. This is time consuming.
- ✓ Library funds spent on UDA materials accessed or purchased is more cost effective. Materials purchased on UDA plans by default get used, and there is evidence to suggest that these materials will continue to have impressive post-purchase usage.
- ✓ Use-driven purchases fill collection gaps that traditional selection can miss, particularly as libraries deal with restrictive book budgets.
- ✓ UDA allows flexibility in balancing the amount of immediate versus long-term collection building as determined by each library.
- ✓ UDA allows faculty, researchers, and other users to participate most often unknowingly with collection building.
- ✓ Deposit accounts required by most UDAs are efficient for accounting and require less staff time to manage than buying materials with individual invoices (e.g., university staff, faculty, and students) and may be held in a password or IP-protected streaming media system.

observed that his company was managing "several hundred" demand-driven acquisition (DDA) programs (Travis, 2015).

Given the popularity of use-driven acquisitions, the issue becomes *how much* should a library employ UDA plans as a complement to traditional collection-building methods, rather than *should* UDA be incorporated? It is important for libraries to strike a balance between the traditional methods of collection development and use-driven acquisitions. It is in the best interest of any library to find a balance that is appropriate for their individual circumstance, so the level of UDA incorporated into collection strategies and budgeting will vary from institution to institution. A library with a more pronounced book budget and a stated mission to build extensive collections across many disciplines may not utilize UDA plans to the extent that a library with a primary commitment to meeting immediate user needs.

Impetus for UDA

It is often the issue of low circulation of print books that spurs libraries to launch use-driven acquisition plans (De Fino and Lo, 2011; Levine-Clark, 2011; Roll, 2013). Even libraries that are reluctant to use book funds for use-driven acquisition plans are hard pressed to justify the use of material budgets to purchase print books that so often show little or no use. Yet, one misgiving for some academic librarians is having users drive the acquisitions to the point where collections become unbalanced and trendy. An argument can be made that what is popular with users today may not be relevant for research or instruction tomorrow and years to come. Additionally, certain holdings are meant to be archival in nature, and many libraries have reasons to build wide and expansive collections in targeted areas. For these collection areas and subholdings, *just in case* is a legitimate and desirable approach.

Revising Collection Strategies

Before incorporating use-driven acquisition planning, it is recommended that libraries of all types review their collection development policies or guidelines for acquiring print and e-books in tandem. Use-driven plans can be an excellent complementary tool for collection strategies, but it is crucial for libraries to set clear goals and objectives. To assist librarians in determining when and how to incorporate UDA plans into collection-building and budgeting strategies, it is helpful to work through a series of questions regarding current policies and material fund allocations.

For example, if a library is already spending funds annually to purchase e-books for a reference collection and would like to increase access but has a limited budget, a suitable strategy might be to use a segment or all of the funds spent on reference e-books to launch an evidence-based acquisition (EBA) plan with a publisher of reference materials. EBA plans are a model offered by publishers to libraries that provide access to a large amount of e-book content, but only a certain portion of the content is purchased. In this scenario, the library meets the goal of enhancing the reference collection by offering a wealth of e-book access to users at a reasonable and predetermined cost. Chapter 5 offers an in-depth analysis of EBA plans.

FIVE QUESTIONS REGARDING COLLECTION STRATEGIES

1. Are your collection objectives and policies up to date? Are they meeting the immediate needs of demanding users while building collections as before?
2. Do you analyze circulation and usage data at your library? Is the use of the print books and e-books acquired on approval plans and by firm ordering justifying the expenditures?
3. Are there areas of specialized collections or strength that the library wishes to continue to build using more traditional acquisitions methods, even if UDA plans are being considered or in operation?
4. Is the allocation or formula for distribution of the materials budget current, balanced, and cost effective?
5. Can you channel funds from existing allocations that can balance the support of UDA with traditional collection building?

Flexibility of UDA

One of the attractive elements of use-driven acquisitions for collection development is flexibility. E-books provide the perfect format for UDA plans, as online access is immediate and seamless. Aggregators, publishers, and book vendors will collaborate with libraries to establish demand-driven acquisition (DDA), patron-driven acquisition (PDA), evidence-based acquisition (EBA), or hybrid plans to meet the scope, content, and budget limitations of each library. A number of use-driven acquisition e-book models can be devised to target specific subject areas or disciplines in the content that is made available to users. If libraries wish to build multiple concurrent UDA plans, mediating with vendors and aggregators is helpful, even essential, in reducing duplication. A growing number of publishers with their own platforms offer libraries e-books through evidence-based acquisitions (EBA). EBA is a variation and alternative to the PDA/DDA model. In EBA, a library partners directly with a publisher. The workflow is simple: the library loads e-book MARC records provided by the publisher into the online catalog with links that allow users to open and read the books on the publisher's platform. Funds are deposited with the publisher, and one or more times a year the libraries select and purchase a portion of the e-books based on usage. Publishers may offer libraries e-books subdivided into specific collections, allowing libraries to target subject areas and reduce the cost of the EBA plan if a library is not interested or cannot afford a publisher's entire portfolio. Publishers may allow libraries to include alternative or additional content and tailor the package to meet a specific collection objective. Larger academic libraries often have more than one UDA project in operation, as certain subjects or publisher content are targeted by each plan.

Incorporating Approval Plans

Many use-driven acquisitions plans are started with a fresh set of parameters developed to complement the traditional methods of print and e-book acquisitions, while a significant number are derived from existing approval and slip-plan parameters (see UF Libraries, 2014, Q9). Using an approval plan as the basis for a UDA plan can simplify implementation, as profiles are already established. It should be noted that a library migrating an approval plan entirely into a UDA program might want to review and broaden the profiles so more content is made available to users. Offering additional content is a feature of UDA that should be maximized whenever possible.

There are variations to adapting approval plans for UDA. At California State University, Fullerton (CSUF), a variation on the approval model has been used with early success (see the first case study at the end of this chapter). Instead of running a traditional approval plan for print books, the library is rolling their approval and slip plan into a "demand-driven-preferred approval plan"; the main goal of the revised plan is to receive as much e-book content from their approval and slip matches as possible (Roll, 2013). Instead of automatically shipping print monographs on approval or sending notification slips to selectors matched from the profiles, for titles that are available as e-books, the book vendor supplies MARC records that are loaded into the library catalog for DDA discovery. For the title matches not available as e-books, the print books are shipped on approval and the slips are sent to the librarians for firm order selection. Consequently, this DDA does not save money for the library per se; rather, it increases the number of e-books being supplied with purchase based on use.

The University of Florida George A. Smathers Libraries has developed a DDA-preferred slip plan (see the second library case study at the end of this chapter). The plan is simple in design: for e-books that match profiles set up across the collection spectrum, MARC records are loaded into the catalog as part of the DDA plan. For e-books that publishers will not make available on DDA, titles that are not issued as e-books, or titles not issued as e-books within a sixty-day window, slips for the matches are supplied to library selectors for firm ordering. This DDA slip plan is essentially reducing the number of print books being purchased while increasing the number of e-books accessed at point of need.

Budgeting for UDA

One of the biggest hurdles facing libraries in implementing long-term use-driven acquisition plans is funding. Many libraries are dedicated to supporting instruction and research activities at their institutions, oftentimes across numerous subject disciplines, with annual materials budgets either flat or in decline. After initial allocations for licensed e-resources, and to a lesser degree the print serial and standing order continuations, libraries must deal with populating materials budgets for monographs, e-books, and other resources from this declining pool of discretionary funds. Restrictive materials budgets can be a hindrance, to say the least, for libraries trying to allocate book budgets and operate use-driven plans. In fact, many libraries cite budget restrictions as one primary reason for not deploying use-driven acquisitions (UF Libraries, 2014, Q19).

Despite some librarians who had misgivings about using a portion of the book budget to fund UDA, the importance of developing a means to fiscally support the plans at a library is crucial, especially long term. Budgeting for patron-driven initiatives "should be understood as part of routine collection building and not viewed as a supplement or special initiative. It is an alternative to librarian selection of content and should be funded as part of the library's overall collection plan" (Johnson, 2013, 130).

Libraries must often find creative ways to fund UDA, either by using one-time funding—modifying approval or slip plans that free up existing funds allocated annually—or by diverting existing revenue streams. There are three budget scenarios for libraries to consider as they develop a funding strategy for financing use-driven acquisition plans: (1) one-time funding for pilots or short-term projects; (2) annual funding for sustained programs; and (3) one-time or sustained funding for collaborative shared initiatives. If a library is operating more than one UDA plan, perhaps one as an ongoing program that is funded annually while also engaged in running a pilot or pilots, then both of the first two scenarios come into play. Occasionally individual or shared UDA plans have time lines that are short term, such as grant-funded projects, while others may have started as one-time pilots, found success, and now require annual appropriations. Libraries involved in collaborative plans—for example, shared e-books DDA with their library consortium—will have to consider sustained funding sources as well.

One-time Funding

One-time funding is the simplest and least threatening to budget managers or selectors. The library sets aside a pot of money, often received from a carry-forward, grant, or windfall funding source, and uses it for a pilot UDA plan. In all these cases, funds for a UDA

ONE-TIME FUNDING OPPORTUNITIES

- Libraries may be presented with funds from a grant, from an endowment, or through donor development.
- Surplus funds may be available when scooped from unspent materials funds at the end of a fiscal year, especially when accounting deadlines are reached and invoices or materials are still in transit. Depositing these funds with a vendor or publisher for a UDA plan allows the libraries to use surplus money from a preceding fiscal year.
- Windfall funds are funds that were not in the original materials allocations. In academic libraries, extra funds may come from the university administration or budget office; in public libraries, a city or county might divert bonus monies from a taxing or fiscal program.

plan can be created or arrive unexpectedly, and a library should be prepared to utilize the bonus. A library can create a "wish list" with an inventory of the type, size, and approximate cost of each UDA plan that is ready to initiate if funding arrives.

Annual Funding

Incorporating ongoing UDA plans into collection strategies will require the development of an accompanying budget proposal. A library may elect to continue to fund short-term UDA plans or pilots with funds squeezed from the annual book budgets. Academic libraries interested in developing long-term UDA plans may have to convince some selectors, administrators, and budget managers that it is a fruitful idea to divert book budget funding each year. Not surprisingly, a large number of libraries are indeed using firm or approval book monies to fund use-driven plans (UF Libraries, 2014, Q14). Ideally, a library can fund the traditional firm orders, approval plans, and blanket order budgets, while also diverting a portion to finance UDA plans.

IDEAS FOR REALLOCATING EXISTING RESOURCE AND BOOK BUDGETS

- Shave off a small percentage from every approval profile or firm-order funds to build a modest central fund to apply to a UDA plan. Use a similar strategy for other formats: for example, use a portion of funding for firm-order purchase of streaming video and/or DVDs that can be diverted for a streaming video UDA.
- Conduct e-journal usage analysis and determine if some of the online journals are worth the annual subscriptions; savings from cancellations can be used for e-journal pay-per-view plans.
- Divert a portion or all funds used annually for e-book subscriptions or package purchases for an evidence-based acquisition plan.

The percentage of a materials budget to use for UDA will differ in every library; some libraries will elect to divert a small percentage of their book budgets to UDA plans, while other libraries may choose to expand on the use-driven approach. A library's collection objectives and available budget will have a huge bearing on the final allocation. The dilemma for many libraries, whether academic, public, or specialized, will be to find a balance in the collection and budget strategies that allows sustained use-driven plans while maintaining traditional collection building.

Reallocating Approval Plan Funds

If a library changes all or part of the traditional slip or approval plans into a UDA workflow, a portion of the allocated budget for the slip and approval purchases could be made available for the new hybrid plan. The funding source—funds allocated for an ongoing approval plan—is already in place in the library's annual budget.

Funding Collaborative Plans

Often administrators will fund participation in use-driven plans as part of a library partnership or consortium. Budgeting for collaborative or shared UDA projects can be demanding to a library's book budget, as it is an additional expense. A group or consortia UDA plan will not save libraries money, but participation can be a relatively cost-effective method for collaborative collection building, as the purchases are shared.

Key Points

Implementing use-driven acquisition is a perfect opportunity for libraries to review and update collection policies as well as budget allocations and strategies. Here are the main points to remember going forward:

- Libraries can incorporate use-driven acquisition but should determine clear objectives that balance the just-in-case and just-in-time approaches, based on the collection missions and budgets at their institution.
- Use-driven acquisitions can be employed by libraries to target specific collections or disciplines.
- The use-driven model is flexible and allows libraries to operate multiple plans that can mix and match DDA, EBA, and other plans, especially if the initiatives are coordinated with vendors, aggregators, and publishers.
- Many libraries are facing restrictive material budgets, but there are creative methods of using one-time funds or reallocating annual budgets for use-driven plans.

After a library has developed objectives for what it would like to accomplish using one or more use-driven acquisition plans, the next step is to select the appropriate vendors or publishers, as discussed in the next chapter.

References

De Fino, Melissa, and Mei Ling Lo. 2011. "New Roads for Patron-Driven E-Books: Collection Development and Technical Services Implications of a Patron-Driven Acquisitions Pilot at Rutgers." *Journal of Electronic Resources Librarianship* 23, no. 4: 327–38. doi:10.1080/1941126x.2011.627043.

Esposito, Joseph. 2012. "Sizing the Market for Patron-Driven Acquisitions (PDA)." *Scholarly Kitchen* (blog). May 8. http://scholarlykitchen.sspnet.org/.

Johnson, Peggy. 2013. *Developing and Managing Electronic Collections: The Essentials*. Chicago: American Library Association.

Levine-Clark, Michael. 2011. "Building a Demand-Driven Collection: The University of Denver Experience." In *Patron-Driven Acquisitions: History and Best Practices*, edited by David A. Swords, 45–60. Berlin: De Gruyter Saur.

Roll, Ann. 2013. "A Demand-Driven-Preferred Approval Plan." In *Charleston Conference Proceedings, 2013*. West Lafeyette, IN: Purdue University. doi:10.5703/1288284315304.

Travis, Gregg. 2015. E-mail to authors. January 28.

University of Florida George A. Smathers Libraries (UF Libraries). 2014. "UDA Library Survey." Last updated August 10, 2015. http://ufdcimages.uflib.ufl.edu/IR/00/00/71/94/00001/UDA_Library_Survey.pdf.

Further Reading

Brinkman Dzwig, Zofia E. 2013. "Innovative Collection Development for E-books at the TU Delft Library." *Information Services and Use* 33, no. 1: 37–39. doi:10.3233/ISU-130686.

Gilbertson, Mary, Elizabeth Chadbourn McKee, and Lutishoor Salisbury. 2014. "Just in Case or Just in Time? Outcomes of a 15-Month Patron-Driven Acquisition of E-Books at the University of Arkansas Libraries." *Library Collections, Acquisitions, and Technical Services* 38, no. 1: 10–20. doi:10.1080/14649055.2014.924072.

Herrera, Gail. 2015. "Testing the Patron-Driven Model: Availability Analysis of First-Time Use Books." *Collection Management* 40, no. 1: 3–16. doi:10.1080/01462679.2014.965863.

Sharp, Steve, and Sarah Thompson. 2010. "'Just in Case' vs. 'Just in Time': E-Book Purchasing Models." *Serials* 23, no. 3: 201–6.

Library Case Study: California State University, Fullerton, Pollak Library

Reporting: Ann Roll, collection development librarian

Type of institution: Public; not a member of the Association of Research Libraries (ARL).

Faculty: 2,000

Students: 38,000, includes 5,300 graduates

Consortium: Member of the California State University (CSU) system; affiliate of the Statewide California Electronic Library Consortium (SCELC).

Colleges/programs/research centers supported: Pollak Library is the sole library on campus supporting nine colleges and programs.

Materials budget: fiscal year (FY) 2013–2014: $2,300,000

Number and Type of Use-Driven Acquisition Plans

- One ongoing DDA e-books plan
- One pilot DDA for streaming video
- One pilot for online reference books
- One plan for purchasing print books requested through interlibrary loan

First UDA plan: The first demand-driven acquisitions plan was built in 2010 with Ebook Library (EBL). To avoid print/e-book duplication, improve profile specificity, and provide more complete catalog records, the demand-driven acquisition plan was later incorporated into the existing approval plan setup with Yankee Book Peddler (YBP); slipped titles available as EBL e-books were added to the DDA pool. At the start of FY 2013–2014, another step was taken by creating a "DDA-preferred" approval plan, in which titles that profiled as either print books or as slips and available as EBL e-books are automatically added to the DDA discovery pool.

Features of the main DDA e-books plan: An e-book is auto-purchased after four short-term loans (STLs). The discovery pool of e-book records has over sixty-eight thousand titles. CSUF library has excluded some types of books, such as textbooks, reprints, and most reference books; also excluded are museum and gallery publications, as the library has a separate approval plan with another vendor for these materials.

Budget: Approximately 5 percent of the annual collection development budget is allocated for UDAs. Allocation for use-driven acquisition plans in FY 2013–2014 was $129,000:

- $92,000 for the main e-books plan (not a pilot; ongoing DDA);
- $10,000 for a streaming-video pilot;
- $20,000 for a Gale Virtual Reference Library (GVRL) e-reference pilot; and
- $7,000 for the purchase of print books that were requested via interlibrary loan.

Reasons for incorporating UDA: One major reason for implementing UDA plans was a 77 percent reduction in the monographs budget from 2006 to 2013. Another was a strong desire to provide as much content electronically as possible, not only due to an increasing number of online courses, but also due to space constraints for physical materials. Studies showing low circulation for print books received on approval propelled the transition to a DDA-preferred approval plan that could provide more content for less expenditure.

Start-Up: The library working with EBL did many trials and tweaking to profiling and record loading; it took approximately six months to get the DDA plan running at full steam. The transition to the DDA-preferred approval plan took some time, which included analysis of the use of print-approval books, assessment of e-book availability in subject areas in which we collect, and meetings with subject librarians to discuss the implications.

UDA workflow and maintenance: The first attempt at DDA in 2010 was set up with a profile created with EBL, rather than via the library's approval plan. After monitoring the auto-purchases over the next two years, it was discovered that the original EBL profile included some publishers of popular and/or juvenile content that was out of scope. This content was removed from the catalog, but no other maintenance has been performed.

Assessment and reporting: For the main UDA plan, the library uses the admin interface of EBL and runs reports as needed, but it does not have a standard schedule set in place. The staff gathers statistics on short-term loans and auto-purchases particularly to monitor costs. For accreditation reports requested from departments or schools, the library will include the number of e-book loans in the relevant subject areas.

Challenges of UDAs: In the case of the initial EBL DDA plan, the challenges were largely technical (creating and correcting the load table to add records to the library catalog and ensuring that library guest users could use purchased e-books without triggering new purchases). In the move to the DDA-preferred approval plan, the challenges were more philosophical. Some subject librarians and faculty continue to express their personal preferences for print books and/or their concerns that e-books do not provide the research capabilities of print, but they understand the potential for monetary savings and increased access.

Branding and marketing: CSUF markets e-books to users through posts on a library blog or the news section on the library website but does not mention DDA as a means to acquire access or purchase.

Consortia UDA plans: The California State University (CSU) system has had three e-book DDA pilots with three different aggregators. CSUF participated in all three, but none are ongoing consortia DDA plans. At least for now, the concentration at the consortium level is on providing access to large e-book packages, rather than supporting DDA.

Success of UDA: The library considers the main DDA e-books plan successful, as it is providing much more content at a significantly lower cost than what was being received on the traditional approval plan. The DDA-preferred approval plan is allowing a limited monograph budget to stretch further.

Library Case Study: University of Florida Smathers Libraries

Reporting: Steven Carrico, acquisitions librarian

Type of institution: Public; land grant; space grant; sea grant

Memberships: Association of Research Libraries (ARL); Association of American Universities (AAU); Center for Research Libraries (CRL)

Faculty: 5,106; **Students**: 49,042, includes 17,000 graduates

Consortium: State University System of Florida (SUS); Association of Southeastern Research Libraries (ASERL)

Colleges/programs/research supported: 16 colleges; 100 undergraduate majors, 200 graduate degree programs; 169 research centers and institutes

Materials budget: FY 2014–2015: $11.6 million; FY 2015–2016: $12.1 million

Number and type of UDA plans: FY 2014–2015: $247,500 in total allocations

UDA budgeting: FY 2014–15: $240,000, representing 36 percent of the total monographs budget

Twelve UDA Plans

- $8,500: Print Books PDA plan (Coutts)
- $35,000: Books on Demand (from interlibrary loan requests) PoD plan
- $50,000: Course Reserves PDA plan

- $20,000: Consortium E-Books DDA plan (Coutts)
- $10,000: E-Books Approval Plan DDA plan (Coutts)
- $50,000: E-Books DDA plan—focusing on STEM + Medicine (EBL)
- $25,000: E-Books EBA plan (Cambridge)
- $5,000: E-Books EBA plan (Gale)
- $5,000: E-Books EBA plan—focusing on STEM + Medicine (Elsevier)
- $25,000: three e-journal article PPV plans
- $9,000: Music Scores + Print Books PDA plan (Harrassowitz)
- $5,000: Streaming-video DDA plan (Kanopy)

Fiscal Year 2015–2016: $250,000 in total allocations; $250,000 representing 37 percent of the total monographs budget

Eleven UDA Plans

- $40,000: Books on Demand (from interlibrary loan requests) PoD plan
- $50,000: Course Reserves PDA plan
- $30,000: Consortium E-Books DDA or EBA plan (not yet determined)
- $60,000: E-Books Approval Plan DDA plan (YBP/ProQuest)
- $25,000: E-Books EBA plan (Cambridge)
- $5,000: E-Books EBA plan (Gale)
- $5,000: E-Books EBA plan—focusing on STEM + Medicine (Elsevier)
- $25,000: E-Books DDA plan—focusing on STEM (T&F/CRC)
- $2,000: one e-journal article PPV plan
- $3,000: Music Scores + Print Books PDA plan (Harrassowitz)
- $5,000: Streaming-video DDA plan (Kanopy)

Reasons for incorporating UDA: Reasons to launch multiple plans: (1) a goal to improve the cost-benefit of materials budgets that are increasingly restrictive—expenditures for e-resource continuations are exceeding 80 percent, while firm order print monograph/e-book funds are in serious decline; (2) studies at other academic libraries and those performed at the University of Florida (UF) show a large percentage of print books are not circulating; (3) the university requires increased justification on effective use of library funding; and (4) the library administration is advocating that collection managers spend more time as instructional liaisons with users and faculty and less time devoted to individual selection of books and resources.

UDA and collections and budget strategies: In 2014, the libraries created a new set of strategic directions for acquiring content that advocates both a print-to-e-resources migration and increased just-in-time collecting approach; the collection policies of the libraries are being revamped and subsequent budgets are being reallocated. The libraries have multiple UDA pilots and plans in operation that are being funded by approval plan funding and from reassigned firm order budgets.

UDA workflow and maintenance: The Smathers Libraries have found UDAs (once established) require less staff time and maintenance than firm order workflows. The acquisitions department works closely with the consortium's central IT organization that handles record loading for the consortia plans. Selectors and staff members are contacted on occasion to assess content received on the EBA and PDA/DDA plans and to help update or revise parameters as needed.

Challenges of UDAs: Budgeting for UDA plans is always a challenge, as materials budgets fluctuate and are generally restrictive for discretionary purchases. Collection development is a challenge as the library attempts to balance traditional collection development in preeminent areas, such as Latin America, Florida history, and Judaica collections; firm ordering from a variety of subject areas; and the just-in-time approach using UDA plans. Technical challenges include minimizing duplication, monitoring discovery records in the catalog, and tracking expenditures for each plan. For the shared DDA and EBA plans, the library groups face additional complications in implementation, ongoing management, and budgeting.

Assessment and reporting: The acquisitions department maintains the UDAs on several fronts. Spreadsheets are used to track fund allocations, deposit accounts, and expenditures for each plan. Cost-and-usage reports for assessing the plans are generated quarterly, or as needed, and usually require some vendor or publisher data or report to be manipulated for specific cost-use summaries for broad or specific subject areas. Generally speaking the vendor reports are inadequate, so require a hybrid approach.

Branding and marketing: UF does not market the e-book UDAs but does promote to a small degree the streaming-video and music score PDA plans.

Shared and consortia UDA plans: UF has been involved in one consortia e-books DDA with eleven libraries participating, a shared DDA plan with two libraries participating, and a shared EBA plan with two libraries participating.

Success of the UDA programs: The UDA programs have been viewed mostly as a success based on content received, usage, and cost. The libraries have acquired thousands of print and e-books over the past nine years from the UDA plans. In addition to print and e-books acquired, over the past two years library users benefited from innovative UDAs that offered e-journal articles, music scores, and streaming videos. Users are mostly unaware of the connection from their use to the purchase (or access) of the resource.

Recommendations: For local plans, start on a small scale and build on the pilots, if applicable. Libraries need to take a primary and an active role when running a sustained UDA plan. These UDA plans require continuous maintenance and monitoring, and the vendors do not have the staff or time dedicated to keep track of each plan.

CHAPTER 3

Working with Vendors and Content Providers

IN THIS CHAPTER

- ▷ Selecting a vendor or content provider
- ▷ Developing communication plans
- ▷ Training and providing support
- ▷ Evaluating the UDA plan
- ▷ Managing expectations and responsibilities

AT A BASIC LEVEL, library book vendors sell materials in assorted formats to libraries through a variety of purchasing models, including use-driven acquisition (UDA). Implementing UDA plans creates several options for librarians. This can be both a blessing and a curse; options mean opportunity for scalable, local customization and competitive pricing, but librarians can soon find themselves buried under information overload. This chapter will provide useful guidelines for maximizing collaboration between librarians and vendors. It begins with an overview of vendor options and offerings, and then presents practical suggestions for how to develop and sustain a harmonious partnership between librarians and vendors regarding responsibilities, performance expectations, and ongoing modification and upkeep of UDA. Two vendor spotlights conclude the chapter.

Selecting a UDA Content Provider

Choosing a vendor when contemplating UDA is no insignificant decision and can be a complex process. Early in the planning stages, you should seek input from librarians and staff members in all departments. What do they view as the most important criteria in vendor selection? Are there any deal breakers? What are the goals of the UDA plan, and how might they affect vendor selection? It is also worthwhile to solicit feedback from peer institutions and other librarians who already have experience in setting up UDA plans. Librarians should reach out to colleagues and friends for advice and should expand their reach to listservs and professional organizations to check on the performance of the vendors in consideration.

Though most libraries choose to partner with vendors, librarians should be aware that other content providers, including aggregators and publishers, often manage their own UDA models. Because most libraries collaborate with vendors when implementing UDA e-book plans, this chapter focuses on the vendor relationship, but it is important to become somewhat familiar with the details of each kind of content provider before making final decisions. UDA provision is constantly evolving, but most libraries currently work with one of the following choices.

Aggregators

Aggregators offer purchase of and access to e-books from a variety of publishers. They also host their own proprietary e-book platforms for searching, viewing, and manipulating content. Because not all publishers will offer their content through every aggregator, librarians cannot be assured of collecting all titles from all publishers under a single supplier. However, because aggregators sell content from multiple publishers, they are able to offer a wide scope of material. Aggregators are also beholden to the digital rights management (DRM) restrictions set in place by individual publishers; this often leads to stricter allowances for printing, downloading, and sharing content. You should also be prepared to navigate DRM from multiple publishers when choosing an aggregator for UDA. Most aggregators offer flexibility in purchasing models, including short-term loans (STLs), evidence-based acquisition (EBA), and "free discovery," in which a mediated or unmediated purchase is initiated after a predetermined amount of usage.

Publishers

Some publishers have broken into the UDA market by offering their own models on their own platforms. Unlike working with vendors or aggregators, publishers control their own DRM, which usually means less restrictive allowances for use and sharing. Publishers tend to withhold some content from aggregators and only offer it through their own platforms, so working directly with the publisher may increase the pool of material. However, libraries with publisher-based plans are limited to the content being released by that publisher. Publishers also tend to offer fewer options for purchasing than do aggregators and vendors, and may not support the technological requirements for STL or free discovery. Some publishers offer UDA through a model known as evidence-based acquisition, in which the library is given access to a collection of titles for a set period of time. After that time period is up, the library purchases only the content that saw the most usage. See chapter 5, "Evidence-Based Acquisitions (EBA)," for details on EBA plans.

Vendors

Working with vendors allows for a broad scope of content as well as value-added support in profile creation, record management, de-duplication, and assessment. Most libraries already collaborate with vendors for collection development needs, whether through approval plans, firm ordering, or standing orders. The same benefits of utilizing a vendor for traditional collection development are true for UDA. Vendors partner with multiple publishers and aggregators to sell their content in a retail-like atmosphere. Librarians can choose among a variety of e-book aggregators and purchasing models. They offer enhanced profiling services to ensure that the best content is funneled downstream to library users. Vendors also help to alleviate the problems of de-duplication, as most libraries will wish to employ multiple aggregator platforms and publishers.

Librarians and staff who are already pleased with the performance of a current vendor may want to stick with who they know. Using a current vendor has its advantages: they are already familiar with the library's operations and collection development practices; they will have a record of purchases and holdings; and they have (hopefully) already established an amicable working relationship with one or multiple people in the library. However, as with any large purchasing decision, it is worthwhile to explore other options. While there may be a large amount of overlap among vendors, some will offer a broader variety of formats (print books, e-books, streaming media, journals, etc.) in specific subject areas or from certain publishers. Some vendors own their own e-book platforms, allowing for greater flexibility in negotiating pricing and DRM. Another consideration is how much money the library plans to spend on UDA. Most vendors require a deposit when setting up UDA plans; some will require a minimum amount of anywhere from $5,000 to $25,000.

When it comes to e-books, most vendors offer a comparable universe of platforms and licensing options. If you are considering a UDA plan with print books, vendors will already have relationships with a variety of scholarly and trade publishers. It is important to remember that the vendor is selling a product and not creating content. They are beholden to the restrictions put in place by various publishers, and thus their licensing options will be limited in some cases to what the publisher will allow. Vendors are also selling e-books on platforms that are not necessarily "owned" by that vendor family. While not entirely comprehensive, the list of vendors in table 3.1 is a helpful starting point of contact.

Once you have narrowed down your potential vendor options, you should be prepared to ask at least the following questions, though each library will have its own goals and priorities:

- Is there a minimum amount of money required for a deposit?
- What is the time line involved in implementing the UDA plan? How long will it be before the plan is up and running?
- Will the vendor provide an on-site visit to help with the technical setup and/or profile creation?
- What is the vendor's plan for ongoing support and training?
- What kinds of usage reports and statistics does the vendor provide?
- What are the allowances for printing, downloading, and sharing electronic content?
- Can the library add and remove MARC records for content throughout the lifespan of the UDA plan?
- Will the vendor provide high-quality MARC records to facilitate discovery?
- Can the vendor assist with de-duplication against what the library already owns?

Table 3.1. List of vendors

VENDOR/PUBLISHER/ AGGREGATOR	MORE INFORMATION	CURRENT UDA PROVIDER?
Cambridge University Press	"For Librarians: Evidence Based Acquisition," http://ebooks.cambridge.org/	Yes, through evidence-based acquisition
EBL/ProQuest	http://www.proquest.com/products-services/EBL-Demand-driven-Acquisition.html	Yes
Ebrary/ProQuest	http://www.ebrary.com/corp/models.jsp#pda	Yes
EBSCO	"Patron Driven Acquisition," http://www.ebscohost.com/	Yes
Gale	"Introducing Our New Usage-Driven Acquisition Model," http://assets.cengage.com/	Yes, for reference
LYRASIS	http://www.lyrasis.org/	Yes
ProQuest Coutts	http://www.proquest.com/products-services/MyiLibrary.html	Yes
Rittenhouse	"Patron Driven Acquisition Now Available from the R2 Digital Library," https://www.rittenhouse.com/	Yes, for Health Sciences
Wiley	"E-books," http://www.wiley.com/	Yes, through evidence-based acquisition
Yankee Book Peddler	"Demand-Driven Acquisitions (DDA)," http://www.ybp.com/	Yes

- Which e-book aggregator and/or publisher platforms does the vendor offer? Which purchasing models are available for UDA plans (STL, EBA, free discovery, etc.)?
- What will the patron-facing display of UDA records look like?

It is practical to designate one librarian as the library representative between the library and potential vendors. This will save time and confusion for both parties. This responsibility usually falls to the head of collection development or acquisitions but could also be the electronic resources librarian or a member of technical services.

If the library shows interest, vendors may offer to conduct on-site visits or webinars to demonstrate their products and services. Because implementing and sustaining UDA plans will involve stakeholders from almost all areas of the library, the library representative should be prepared to share information, solicit questions and concerns, and communicate answers in a timely manner. In order to keep track of ongoing tasks and responsibilities, you may want to develop a simple communication plan using project management tools or checklists.

The next steps involve developing the consideration pool, or discovery pool, to be included in the UDA plan. This might include working with a vendor to create a profile, or at least choosing among subject collections. Most libraries rely on their vendor when selecting the parameters of the UDA plan (UF Libraries, 2014, Q9). Before any profiling work can be done, librarians need to solidify how much money they plan to commit to UDA. Some intrepid libraries have shifted their entire collection development budgets to UDA, but most libraries opt to redeploy only a percentage of their funds for UDA (UF Libraries, 2014, Q15). Libraries are in the habit of making do with less every year as budgets shrink and print circulation drops. In the reverse, it is not uncommon for libraries to have acquisitions funds left over at the end of a fiscal year, or to receive a gift or endowment to be used for collection development. UDA can act as a practical way to make the most of shrinking budgets *and* unexpected windfalls.

A library should work with a vendor to determine the optimal size of the consideration pool. At this point profiling begins, and depending on the size and complexity of the program, the vendor might visit the library to conduct profiling sessions or may gather all the necessary information via phone or e-mail. Most vendors will offer to send templates of their profiling documents to help librarians prepare for a meeting. The templates can also be used to create the profiles themselves, with the librarians filling in the appropriate information and sending them back to the vendor, without the need for a formal meeting.

Record Delivery and Profile Activation

Activating the UDA plan will be a multistep process, and libraries should set up specifications with their vendor early in the implementation stages. If the library chooses to load MARC records to enhance the discoverability of their UDA plan content, the following should be discussed among the librarians and technical services team and communicated to the vendor:

- Are there any special signifiers or fields that should be included in the UDA records that will make them identifiable from others?
- How often should the library receive files of UDA records once the profile is activated?
- What is the library's ideal method of record delivery?
- Does the library want to receive enhanced records when UDA titles are purchased?
- Is there an extra cost from the vendor associated with enhanced records?
- What is the best method for removing records?
- How often will records be removed?

Training

Libraries implementing UDA plans may not already be familiar with the various platforms and systems they and their users will encounter. Librarians or their library representative should request demonstrations and training sessions either in person or through webinars on how to access and maneuver through the content of their UDA plans. Library users expect their librarians to be experts on the use of their resources, and they will need guidance on how to navigate e-book, e-journal, or streaming media platforms and digital rights management for one or multiple providers. The librarian responsible for management of the UDA plan may need training on administrative functions. Vendors should be willing to provide initial training and ongoing support when needed.

Evaluation, Assessment, and Support

Once the profile has been activated, the records loaded, and the content "switched on," it is time to let the UDA plan go to work. Users should be given time to discover and access UDA content, but this does not mean that the library-vendor relationship is at an end. After the program is up and running, it is more important than ever for the library to be in contact with their vendor regarding any issues that cannot be resolved locally. Communication is the most important element in a successful, ongoing relationship between libraries and vendors. The "library representative" should confirm that their vendor offers customer service through multiple channels (telephone, e-mail, online chat, etc.) and that the representatives will be available during reasonable business hours.

Perhaps the most important reason for ongoing contact is the need for evaluation and assessment. As stated in the National Information Standards Organization (NISO)'s Recommended Practice on "Demand Driven Acquisition of Monographs," "Assessment should be an integral part of any DDA program and should be considered early in the planning process" (2014, 23). Vendors are also aware of the importance of usage assessment and the need for improvement. As Bob Nardini, vice president of library services at ProQuest Coutts, states, "We need to make reporting more routine, and we need to make it easier for librarians to run routine reports themselves" ("Vendor Spotlight: Coutts Information Services"). Data resulting from the potential success or failure of any new collection development initiative will be used to inform future practices. Evidence of success can justify the time spent on implementation and can make the case for ongoing funding. Libraries most often collect and analyze usage data in the following ways: in-house reporting, COUNTER reports, and vendor/aggregator-supplied reporting.

In-house reporting: some libraries collect usage statistics without vendor input by running reports through their integrated library system (ILS). The drawback to this method is that the vendor will have additional data elements that go beyond what the local ILS can provide, so the library is limited to a set of data that may not pertain to UDA usage.

COUNTER reports (http://www.projectcounter.org/): COUNTER was developed to standardize the way usage is collected and reported for electronic resources, such as e-books and e-journals. The benefit is the ability to compare usage statistics across platforms and among various providers, but the drawback is the inability to tailor reports for UDA usage. COUNTER reports will also not include pricing data.

Vendor/aggregator-supplied reporting: The majority of libraries either generate or request vendor-supplied usage reports (UF Libraries, 2014, Q11). Aggregator websites will offer some level of reporting that can be requested or created by the library. If the UDA plan consists of titles from one single aggregator, it may be easier for the library to request reports directly from the aggregator rather than a vendor. However, if the UDA plan consists of titles from a variety of aggregators, reporting may come directly from the aggregators or from the vendor.

According to Kristine Baker, director of digital sales at Yankee Book Peddler (YBP), because vendors usually do not manage the e-book platforms themselves, customers receive usage data on DDA activity directly from aggregators or publishers ("Vendor Spotlight: YBP Library Services"). Vendor and aggregator-supplied reports will have the added benefit of including pricing information as well as traditional use and purchasing statistics. Most will list valuable data on usage that goes beyond what has been purchased, including time spent in the book, page views, downloads, and the number of STLs. One of the most significant pieces of information the vendor can provide is how many times the title was used after purchase. While vendor and aggregator-supplied reports will provide a wealth of data beyond what the ILS and COUNTER can display, the reports will not be standardized and thus may require some formatting and editing before being analyzed.

If the library is planning to rely on their vendor for usage reports, they must communicate their needs early in the process. Not all vendors and aggregators will have the mechanisms in place to collect the kind of data the library needs, so the library should be prepared to use a variety of reporting methods. Vendors may still be in the developmental stages of creating reports to support the latest UDA plans (consortia, print, etc.), and they will welcome input from the library on which data elements should be included.

When the UDA plan has been operating for six months to one year, depending on the size of the UDA plan and the needs of the library, you and your vendor should work together to evaluate the program. Most large, research-intensive institutions should expect a vendor evaluation twice a year, while medium-sized or smaller libraries should expect an evaluation annually. During the evaluation, vendor representatives should meet with the librarians who are active in UDA planning and maintenance to analyze usage data. The librarians should be prepared to voice concerns and to request changes to the program if needed. The vendor should provide analysis of the past usage and make recommendations for improvements. The vendor collection specialist may also participate in the evaluation to determine if any adjustments should be made to the profile(s).

Although a formal evaluation will take place once or twice in a year, librarians should not horde questions or grievances throughout the year. These should be addressed as they arise so the vendor can fix issues and implement resolutions at the point of need.

Managing Expectations

Libraries who have been partnering with vendors for collection development initiatives may already be familiar with the kinds of tasks, one-time and ongoing, for which each party should take responsibility. Librarians who are not familiar with the roles and responsibilities inherent in the library/vendor relationship should address this with their vendor representative early in the UDA planning process. This communication and shared expectation will result in a more efficient and gratifying experience for everyone involved. Table 3.2 lists the expected responsibilities of both the vendor and the librarian when planning, implementing, and maintaining UDA plans, though individual experiences will differ.

Key Points

Implementing UDA is an opportunity for libraries to develop or strengthen their vendor relationships. Here are some key points to remember:

- Vendor selection is a multistep process, and the decision should involve stakeholders throughout the library and the community.

Table 3.2. Library/vendor responsibilities

LIBRARY RESPONSIBILITIES	VENDOR RESPONSIBILITIES
• Provide vendor with main library representative and any other librarian contacts.	• Provide library with list of contacts for each area of service (customer service, sales, technical support, etc.).
• Communicate issues and concerns as they arise.	• Resolve issues and technical difficulties.
• Provide vendor with information on degree programs, areas of study, etc. in conjunction with profile creation.	• Conduct profiling session in person, via phone, or via e-mail to determine parameters. Provide title lists before activating profiles.
• Deliver local holdings information to vendor in order to prevent duplication (optional).	• De-duplicate UDA records against library holdings (if provided to vendor).
• Instruct library patrons on use of e-book platforms.	• Conduct training and perform demonstrations on e-book platforms and other pertinent products.
• Inform library patrons of DRM restrictions when appropriate.	• Inform library of DRM restrictions for each publisher/aggregator.
• Provide vendor with budgetary information.	• Guide library and offer advice on estimated rate of spend.
• Inform vendor of the usage data the library will need to collect.	• Make usage statistics and other appropriate data available through website and/or upon request from the library.
• Ensure UDA records are discoverable through the OPAC, discovery service, and/or aggregator platform.	• Send quality MARC records for UDA titles to library (including order-level records) for initial and subsequent loads.
• Notify vendor immediately if any UDA records are removed.	• Notify library immediately if any UDA records must be removed.
• Stay informed and up to date by attending webinars and other training opportunities.	• Inform library of ongoing webinars, tutorials, training sessions, and advisory group opportunities.
• Participate in annual or biannual evaluation.	• Conduct annual or biannual evaluation.
• Monitor usage and spend rates and notify vendor as needed.	• Monitor usage and notify library when approaching spend limit.

- Partnering with a vendor gives the library value-added advantages such as a superior pool of content through the use of profiles, record delivery and removal, and training on various systems and platforms.
- Vendors can facilitate the evaluation and assessment of UDA through ongoing data collection and analysis.
- The library-vendor partnership will be most effective through frequent communication and frank discussion.

In the next chapter, the focus will shift to implementing and managing a "demand-driven acquisition (DDA) plan," the most prevalent UDA model for acquiring e-books.

References

NISO (National Information Standards Organization). 2014. "Demand Driven Acquisition of Monographs: A Recommended Practice of the National Information Standards Organization." June 24. http://www.niso.org/.

University of Florida George A. Smathers Libraries (UF Libraries). 2014. "UDA Library Survey." Last updated August 10, 2015. http://ufdcimages.uflib.ufl.edu/IR/00/00/71/94/00001/UDA_Library_Survey.pdf.

Further Reading

Baker, Kristine, and Ann-Marie Breaux. 2013. "The Evolution of Academic Book Vendor Services for eBooks." *Against the Grain* 25, no. 2: 20–24.

Brooks, Sam. 2006. "Introduction: The Importance of Open Communication Between Libraries and Vendors." *Library/Vendor Relationships* 44, nos. 3/4: 1–4.

Brooks, Stephen M. 2013. "What's Next for E-book Acquisitions? Challenges for Libraries, Vendors, and Publishers." *Against the Grain* 25, no. 2: 26–28.

Carlson, David H. 2006. "Introduction: Forging Lasting Symbiotic Relationships between Libraries and Vendors." *Library/Vendor Relationships* 44, no. 3: 5–10.

Coe, George. 2006. "Managing Customer Relationships: A Book Vendor Point of View." *Library/Vendor Relationships* 44, nos. 3/4: 43–55.

Downey, Kay. 2014. "Technical Services Workflow for Book Jobber-Mediated Demand Driven E-book Acquisitions." *Technical Services Quarterly* 31, no. 1: 1–12. doi:10.1080/07317131.2014.844617.

Draper, Daniel C. 2013. "Managing Patron-Driven Acquisitions (PDA) Records in a Multiple Model Environment." *Technical Services Quarterly* 30, no. 2: 153–65.

Emery, Jill, and Bonnie Parks. 2012. "The Demand Driven Acquisitions Pilot Project by the Orbis Cascade Alliance: An Interview with Members of the Demand Driven Acquisitions Implementation Team." *Serials Review* 38, no. 2 (June): 132–36. doi:10.1016/j.serrev.2012.04.008.

Riley, John D. 2010. "Library Marketplace—Patron Driven Acquisitions from the Point of View of a Traditional Vendor." *Against the Grain* 22, no. 5: 78–79.

Westfall, Micheline, Justin Clarke, and Jeanne M. Langendorfer. 2013. "Selecting a Vendor: The Request for Proposal (RFP) from Library and Vendor Perspectives." *Serials Librarian* 64, nos. 1–4: 188–95.

Vendor Spotlight: ProQuest Coutts

Interview with: Bob Nardini, vice president of product development

What formats do you offer for UDA? Print and e-book.

Do you offer options for consortia UDA? We do. We work with some consortia for PDA.

Do you have a formula or methodology in place to estimate rate of spend? We can always cite the experience of other libraries and groups, but circumstances vary over time. Budgets change. Different users have different preferences. Library A may be different from library B. We can say what we've found to be "normal," but there's no perfect way of predicting how expenditures are going to go. We do help libraries to monitor expenditures against library budgets and are developing an automated mechanism to alert libraries when spending thresholds are approaching.

What are some of the challenges of implementing UDA from the vendor perspective?

- Controlling the spending is definitely one. You need a way to quickly and efficiently shut off the content and quickly turn it back on when the money is refreshed.
- Another is the need to be in frequent contact with many publishers over their policies and terms for UDA, which vary from publisher to publisher, and are not necessarily static with any given publisher. So, we have to not only be in control of the mechanics of what we're working with but also be talking to the publishers and be able to switch things on and off, or back and forth, or in and out, according to what the publishers are deciding—and sometimes decisions change—about prices, about allowable license models, and about UDA itself. This has really forced aggregators and publishers to have more contact than what they've had in the past.
- Print PDAs. I'm seeing a growing interest in print PDAs, and in order to do that you have to be able to fill an order in a reasonable amount of time. It's an opportunity for vendors who have a lot of inventory to fine-tune and adjust their stocking mechanisms. Right now, though, expectations are sometimes beyond what any vendor can deliver. We expect that the continued growth of print-on-demand publishing will make print PDA programs more routine in the future.
- Vendors have to have very close relationships with libraries. If libraries want to purge their pool of records, for example, we have to have effective mechanisms to do that efficiently, so that what we think is available to their user community actually is available and that anything in fact no longer available, perhaps because of a changed publisher policy, comes out of the library's pool of MARC records. By fits and starts, we have improved this over the years, and we expect to continue improving in the years ahead.

Do you offer usage reporting to your UDA customer libraries? Yes, although again, we expect to continue improving what we offer to libraries. We need to make reporting more routine, and we need to make it easier for librarians to run routine reports themselves. Sometimes this would mean developing new reports accessible to users, and sometimes it would mean more training for librarians in the reports already available. One example of a reporting improvement would be this: with all the data in various vendor repositories, there ought to be a way to put that data to use to say more easily than we can today what the "typical" library experience is.

Are there situations in which you would not recommend UDA? If the budget is very unstable, especially if it's a very small library without much budget to start with. Also, perhaps in subject areas where e-books are less common, especially one where there's a high risk of a book quickly becoming unavailable. In general, though, no, I think PDA is becoming or is a standard component of academic libraries.

How do you see UDA evolving in the next five years? Publishers are nervous; "what's it going to do to our sales?" Instead of looking at PDA as a way to sell books, they might look at it as a way to market books, and so increase sales. If vendors and publishers work together, put together something more resembling what users are used to seeing on Amazon instead of a MARC record, publishers able to do that would have an edge. The OPAC is the heart for discovery of PDA programs. There ought to be a place where members of the college community would be able to find and access PDA books not confined to catalogs. That might be departmental websites that tie back into the library. A member of the faculty or a student looks for a book, sees if the library owns it, and accesses it or orders it (depending upon format) if it isn't owned.

I remember a visit I made to a library in Scotland. Things work differently in the UK, wherein many of the libraries, selection never was a principal duty of the librarians. It was the academic faculty's job. This library is a very large library, well known, and receives something like ten thousand individual book requests per year. This was all manual, no system to control it. That's PDA, for sure, but not as we know it. This library really could have used a more efficient recommendation system resembling what we know as "PDA." And libraries here in North America could use better recommendation systems that are not confined to the OPAC's PDA. Patrons should have other ways of telling the library what books they need.

Vendor Spotlight: YBP Library Services

Interview with: Kristine Baker, director of digital sales

What formats do you offer for UDA? Print and e-books.

Do you offer options for consortia UDA? Yes, we have worked on a number of demand-driven acquisition consortia projects. Each project is unique in what content is offered, what publishers agree to participate, and what e-book platform is used for the program. We offer our demand-driven acquisition (DDA) service through our e-book partners.

Do you have a formula or methodology in place to estimate rate of spend? Based on our experience with other DDA programs, we can assist with determining the approximate rate of spend for DDA programs. A number of factors contribute to the spend rate, including the size of the institution or consortium members, the number of titles in the program, the use of short-term loans or not, and how discoverable the content is to the library patrons (OPAC, Discovery Layer, or both). YBP and our e-book partners offer reports to assist with monitoring spend rates for each customer.

What are some of the challenges of implementing UDA from the vendor perspective? The biggest challenge for YBP was developing an integrated service that worked with our e-book partners. It required substantial work and coordination of efforts between both parties. We opted to release the new service in phases to allow us the ability to make changes as the service grew. Our first phase was released in early 2011, followed by phase two and three later that year. This first year, as with any new service or product offering, was a learning experience for all parties: YBP, our e-book partners, and our customers. We spent substantial time introducing the service to our customers and providing training on how the service worked in relation to the customer's other services with YBP. We now have three years of experience, and it's become just one of the many services we provide. We offer the option for customers to choose one e-book supplier or multiple e-book suppliers for their DDA program, ensuring duplication control across suppliers so that only one instance of a title is made available for DDA. Today YBP views DDA as a "mainstream" service offering; utilizing our profiling tools, we provide DDA profiles that are customizable per library, much the same as we have done for years with our approval and notifications service. In addition, we have a very good working relationship with our e-book partners, which is critical to the success of all the e-book services we provide.

Do you offer usage reporting to your UDA customer libraries? Usage reports for DDA activity are provided to customers via the supplier chosen for DDA.

How often do you review PDA programs at your customer libraries? YBP reviews DDA programs on a regular basis as we do with our other service offerings to ensure the program is working as expected for the customer.

Are there situations in which you would not recommend UDA? YBP supports DDA and will assist libraries in the process of implementing a new program, offering suggestions and guidance based on our experience with other customers. DDA is most effective as an acquisition method to acquire peripheral content, to expose patrons to content that may not be bought by the library but is available when needed. Many customers choose to use DDA in conjunction with an e-approval plan and single-title orders as a complement to what is bought by the library. E-packages are another valuable source of content and can be purchased through YBP where workflow support (including duplication control) is provided for the purchase.

Do you consider PDA to be a successful acquisitions model? Yes, we continue to receive requests for this service option, and in combination with our other acquisitions models it has proven to be a success for many of our customers.

How do you see UDA evolving in the next five years? I believe we are only at the beginning of how this service will evolve; as libraries, publishers, and vendors have more data to analyze on the impact of this new model, I expect to see changes in how the model is used by libraries and what type of content is part of this acquisition model. There are many discussions about the impact of DDA and what the long-term effect will be for the library. Is the money spent purely for access and not ownership? What does this mean for the library collection? And is this model one that is sustainable for publishers and suppliers?

Part 2

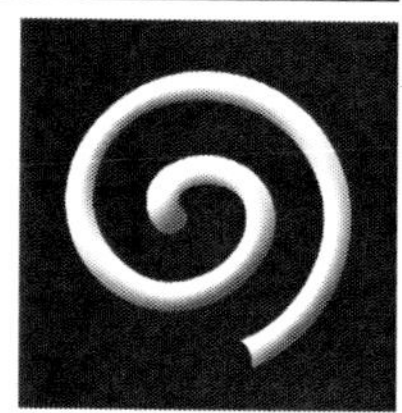

E-BOOK UDA PLANS

CHAPTER 4

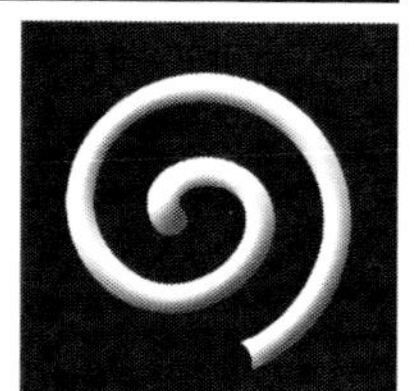

Demand-Driven Acquisitions (DDA)

IN THIS CHAPTER

- ▷ Choosing e-book selection models and content providers
- ▷ Developing and designing an e-book DDA plan
- ▷ Managing the DDA e-book project

E-BOOKS ARE A POPULAR FORMAT FOR use-driven acquisition (UDA). Libraries have adopted this model with increasing vigor since the first demand-driven acquisition (DDA) model was introduced by NetLibrary in the late 1990s (Nixon, Freeman, and Ward, 2011). As demand for e-books rises, and as e-books become available simultaneously with their print counterparts, e-book DDA plans are becoming commonplace among libraries of all sizes.

This chapter will focus on the planning and implementation of e-book DDA plans. It begins with an overview of the landscape of e-book selection models and content providers that offer DDA options, factors to consider when developing an e-book DDA plan, and useful tips for project management. At the end of the chapter, three case studies demonstrate how academic libraries of differing sizes approached this model.

Selection Models and Content Providers

The landscape of e-book acquisition is no longer as simple as it was in the 1990s. Content providers offer countless licensing and selection models that can be blended and interrelated to form a complex web for DDA of e-books. Options are welcome, as they provide more opportunity for libraries of all sizes and collection goals to put DDA into practice, but they can also be daunting. Once a library commits to an e-book DDA, the staff works with the content provider to determine which selection models work best to

REASONS LIBRARIES SHOULD IMPLEMENT E-BOOK DDA PLANS

- ✓ Use-driven e-books are offered just in time not just in case.
- ✓ Vendors and aggregators develop DDA e-book plans specific to a library's collection and budget strategies.
- ✓ Libraries can offer thousands of e-books to users; only those that are used are loaned or purchased.
- ✓ Many e-books will be used repeatedly, some heavily.
- ✓ DDA e-book plans can be a cost-effective use of library funds.
- ✓ The technical workflow can become more streamlined than with traditional firm ordering.
- ✓ Parameters of the plan can be set to customize content for all types and sizes of libraries.
- ✓ Purchased e-books fill in gaps that may have been missed by traditional title-by-title selection.

Table 4.1. E-book DDA selection models

SELECTION MODEL	PROS	CONS
Preset publisher packages (e.g., Wiley, Oxford University Press)	• May include "premium" content the publisher does not allow through aggregators. • Less restrictive **DRM** when working directly with publisher. • Will usually involve a one-time record load.	• Content pool is limited to specific publisher(s). • Publisher may remove content at its discretion.
Preset subject collections (e.g., Ebrary Academic Complete)	• Includes content from a variety of publishers. • Can choose subject collections that reflect institutional goals and programs. • Will usually involve a one-time record load.	• Publishers may withhold "premium" content from collections. • Titles may move in and out of collections each year.
Profile-based (multiple vendors and/or aggregators)	• Profile(s) can be customized to generate content that fits the goals of the UDA. • Profile parameters can be modified at any time to include and exclude content. • Content pool can include titles from multiple publishers and aggregators. • Newly published titles are added regularly.	• Publishers may withhold "premium" content from vendors and aggregators. • Publishers may remove content at their discretion. • DRM may be different for each publisher and will be more restrictive. • Requires an ongoing technical services workflow for record loading, maintenance, and removal.

achieve the goals of the library's program. Though each content provider will offer their own options (and combinations of options), most libraries choose one of the selection models shown in table 4.1.

Choose a selection model (or models) that reflects the goals of your library's DDA program. Most libraries choose to partner with a vendor and/or e-book aggregator, as they offer a wide universe of content and time-saving, customizable services. Once it is decided how to select DDA content, explore the varying licensing models. Each publisher and e-book aggregator offers its own proprietary licensing models, though most offer some variation of the models found in table 4.2. Ask the vendor or aggregator to demonstrate their most up-to-date models.

Librarians need to have a solid understanding of how their patrons use (or do not use) e-books before deciding on licensing levels. Institutions that experience high e-book usage may want to explore multiuser or access models in order to prevent turnaways (a title that displays but is not accessible through the plan). At institutions where users have not had previous access to or have not adopted use of e-books, single-user licensing may be adequate. E-books that will be used heavily for a course or that are part of a distance-learning program will require multiuser access.

Another advantage of collaborating with a vendor or aggregator is that libraries will not be limited to choosing one single licensing model for the entire DDA plan. This is particularly important, as not all e-book titles (even from the same publisher) will be offered at the same licensing level. These decisions are made by publishers on a title-by-title basis, so it is difficult to predict which content will be available at what licensing level. The vendor may ask a library to complete documentation ranking first, second, and even third choices for how to purchase e-books through your DDA. Remember to keep the goals and budget of the DDA plan in mind when determining licensing models, but also note that once the plan is up and running modifications are acceptable.

Table 4.2. E-book DDA licensing models

	SINGLE USER (ONE USER AT A TIME)	MULTIUSER (THREE OR MORE SIMULTANEOUS)	UNLIMITED USER (UNLIMITED USERS AT THE SAME TIME)	"ACCESS" MODELS (PRESET NUMBER OF USES ON A SINGLE TITLE PER YEAR)	SHORT-TERM LOANS	OTHER
Ebrary*	Yes	Yes: 3 user	Yes: multiple user	No	Yes	**Extended access** model for single-user titles
EBSCO	Yes	Yes: 3 user	Yes	Yes: 365 uses	Yes	
MyiLibrary	Yes	Yes	No	Yes: access model, 365 uses	Yes	
EBL*	No	Yes: textbook model	Yes	Yes: nonlinear lending, 325 uses	Yes	**Short-term circulation** for single use

* Note: Ebrary and EBL are now part of ProQuest.

Libraries should also consider whether or not to include short-term loans (STLs). This model has increased in popularity as libraries shift their focus from ownership of e-books to access. With STLs, instead of immediately purchasing the content used in a DDA plan, users are "loaned" full access to the content for a predetermined amount of time (usually with options from one to twenty-eight days). Libraries pay a set percentage of the list price of the e-book with each loan. The percentage paid may increase with each newly triggered loan. After a title has been loaned for a preset number of times, the library may purchase the e-book, but the costs of each loan do not factor into the final purchase price of the title. So, the library may end up paying a significant amount above the original list price of the title.

Publishers are in a constant state of flux over setting prices for STLs. Though DDA can be cost effective for libraries, it presents a different story for publishers who are no longer able to guarantee steady revenue from title-by-title print monograph purchasing. In the face of shrinking and uncertain profits, many publishers have significantly raised their STL prices. This forces libraries to adjust their DDA practices by lowering their price caps, reducing their loan periods, or turning off STLs entirely. Libraries considering STLs will need to consult with their vendor to determine current publisher rates and to ask if they anticipate future price hikes. Also, STL is yet another purchasing option and not a mandate. Some libraries, including Rollins College, choose not to use STLs at all and instead purchase all e-books accessed through DDA (see the first library case study at the end of the chapter).

Profile Creation

Once libraries have worked with their content provider to decide on purchasing and licensing models, profile creation may begin. Depending on the size of the institution, the DDA budget, existing library resources, and the goals of the plan, profiling can be relatively simple or complex. Instead of reinventing the wheel, many libraries with existing approval plans opt to repurpose them to function as the mechanism by which e-book DDA records are generated. Several libraries, including Nova Southeastern University (NSU), are finding success with integrating their DDA endeavors into currently functioning approval profiles, by which titles published within a specific time frame automatically become part of the plan (see the second library case study). Still other libraries choose to scrap their existing approval profiles to start from scratch with DDA profiles (UF Libraries, 2014, Q9).

Once the budget for the DDA program is determined, the next step is to decide on how much content to add to the plan. Content providers can make educated suggestions for libraries based on past experience with other libraries, but as of yet, there is no guaranteed recipe for determining how quickly the DDA budget will be spent. If libraries are too conservative in their approach, they may experience low usage and spending. If they are too liberal, they may spend their UDA funds too quickly, or even overspend. The best way for librarians to approach this decision is to consider institutional factors and their own priorities for what they hope to accomplish with the DDA program.

Because the relationship between size of the DDA program and rate of spend is nebulous at best, many libraries, such as the Kent State University Libraries, choose to start with a pilot program (Downey, 2014) where they commit only a small amount of money to the DDA program and focus on a smaller pool of content. A pilot program

FACTORS TO CONSIDER WHEN DETERMINING RATE OF SPEND FOR DDA BUDGET

- Amount of money to spend
  - A generous budget will necessitate a larger pool of content with potentially higher title-by-title list prices. A modest budget will necessitate a narrower pool of content with lower title-by-title prices.
- Enrollment
  - A larger full-time enrollment (FTE) will mean a wider pool of users, while a smaller FTE will mean fewer potential users.
- Current usage (if any)
  - If the library already offers e-books and has experienced high adoption in the past, librarians can assume that this DDA content will also see high usage. If the library has not offered e-books in the past, or has offered them but has experienced low usage, librarians can assume that DDA titles may also see low usage, at least at the beginning of the program.
- Degree programs
  - Libraries at institutions that offer a wide range of degree programs and interdisciplinary areas of study will want to include a variety of titles in the DDA pool. Libraries at institutions that offer limited degree programs, or branch or special libraries (music, law, health sciences, etc.) will want to offer a more targeted pool of content.
- Level of librarian intervention
  - Some libraries do not expect librarian intervention when selecting titles for the DDA plan, which can open the door to a wider variety. Other libraries will choose content for DDA based on librarian selection, which may have the effect of narrowing the content.

runs for a set amount of time, and then usage is analyzed before committing to a more full-fledged DDA plan. A comprehensive pilot program should run for one full academic year, as usage will undoubtedly rise and fall with the requirements of the academic calendar. For more on the value of a pilot see chapter 1, "Use-Driven Acquisition Project Management."

Preparing for the Profiling Session

Before meeting with the vendor representative, librarians should solicit input from the faculty members in their subject departments. Faculty members may have their own preferences for publishers, editions, and so forth, that can both inform the profiling process and help the librarian to prepare. It is also practical to consult any existing library collection development policies, though many libraries choose to amend their policies in light of implementing DDA.

Profiling for e-book UDA is similar to profiling for an approval or slip-notification profile but with some differences:

Traditional versus Contemporary Philosophy. The collection philosophy behind DDA is different than that of a traditional approval plan. Approval plans are meant to control and limit the content acquired by the library through a set of parameters. DDA plans are meant to *broaden* the scope of content available to a library and its patrons. Librarians should approach DDA profiling with the intent of expanding their traditional collection development offerings to include formats, publishers, and subjects that they may not have included in their approval profiles.

Keep an Open Mind. DDA, at its core, is intended to fulfill real-time patron needs and not the perceived needs of patrons based on librarian subject expertise. This is not to downplay the vital role of the subject specialist but rather to enhance the richness of the library collection with titles that have guaranteed usage and proven interest to patrons. With this in mind, librarians should approach DDA profiling with the understanding that a profile with overly restrictive parameters may compromise the success of the DDA plan.

Librarians should not hesitate to ask their vendor what kind of information they should bring to a profiling session. Some sessions will be simple and straightforward, and others can involve complex back-and-forth negotiations to reach satisfactory parameters. Librarians can use the checklist in table 4.3 to make sure they have given forethought to the parameters that will most likely be addressed in a profiling session, though each vendor will have its own approach. Regardless of the level of complexity, most profiling sessions will cover the following parameters: price cap, subjects, and nonsubject parameters.

Table 4.3. Profile prep checklist

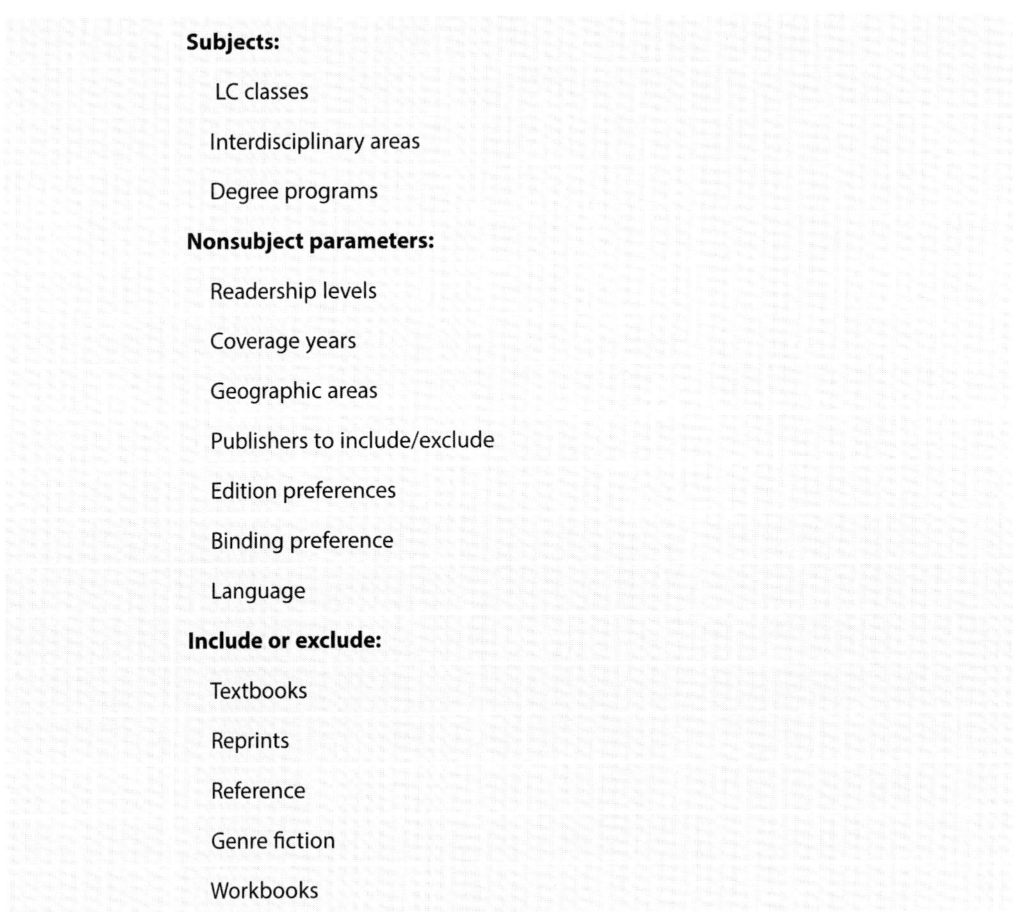

Subjects:

- LC classes
- Interdisciplinary areas
- Degree programs

Nonsubject parameters:

- Readership levels
- Coverage years
- Geographic areas
- Publishers to include/exclude
- Edition preferences
- Binding preference
- Language

Include or exclude:

- Textbooks
- Reprints
- Reference
- Genre fiction
- Workbooks

Price Cap

All DDA plans should include a price cap. Titles equal to or below the price cap that match all other parameters of the DDA profile will become part of the pool of content. Titles above that price cap will not match the profile, or in some cases, will be sent as slip notifications instead. Determining a satisfactory price cap will depend on factors such as which subjects are included and how much the library has to spend on DDA. At the University of North Carolina at Chapel Hill (UNC-CH), a large, public research university, DDA purchases are integrated into a $1.5 million per year acquisitions budget, allowing for a more generous price cap at $250 per title (see the third library case study). At Rollins College, a small, private liberal arts college, the DDA budget is considerably smaller, and thus the price cap is set at $100 per title (see the first library case study). Some subjects (particularly in the STEM disciplines) have a higher average list price per title than others. You should work with your vendor to identify the average list prices of e-books in your profiled subject areas and then apply these to each profile. If creating one single profile for all subject areas in the plan, vendors may still be able to assign differing price caps to each subject range, or even to different publishers.

Subjects

Classification Based

Most vendors now create profiles based on classification systems such as the Library of Congress (http://www.loc.gov/) or National Library of Medicine (http://www.nlm.nih.gov/). This is advantageous for librarians, as most will have some familiarity with the classification of their subject areas. This also makes usage data on subject areas easier to analyze.

Interdisciplinary Aspects

An advantage of DDA is the ability to expand the scope of the record pool, or discovery pool, beyond what may be picked up through an approval plan or slip notifications. One way to accomplish this is to consider material of an interdisciplinary nature. This will not only widen the scope of material included in DDA, thus increasing activity, but also make librarians aware of the kind of material their patrons will use when presented with a greater variety.

Nonsubject Parameters

Some nonsubject parameters, such as publisher, readership level, and edition, will have a greater effect on profile output than others. While it is important to come prepared with some knowledge of the collection needs of the institution, librarians should not hesitate to rely on the expertise of their vendor's collection specialist when determining what to include and exclude from a DDA profile.

Publication Dates

Most traditional approval and slip profiles are meant to collect newly published e-book titles or new editions. The DDA profile can generate MARC records for both newly published and retrospective titles that match the profile parameters. In order to widen the pool of DDA records, librarians should consider adding retrospective titles from at least the past two to three years, depending on the subject areas.

Publishers

Before considering publishers, librarians should ask their vendor if there are any publishers that do not participate in DDA; most publishers are now on board with use-driven models, but there are still some that withhold content. Deciding on publishers to include in a DDA profile will have a significant impact on the kind of material the profile generates. Most libraries implementing DDA will want to include a variety of publishers in order to maximize the record pool and to provide the widest scope of material to their users. In that case, they will want to partner with an aggregator or vendor, as they ingest e-book content from thousands of publishers and multiple e-book platforms. If a library purchases e-books through publisher packages, such as UNC-CH, the decision may be made to exclude those publishers entirely from the profile (see the third library case study).

Readership Levels

Readership level is another parameter that will have a substantial effect on the scope and volume of UDA titles. Each vendor will have its own unique terminology when denoting readership levels, but most fall into the following categories:

- Graduate/doctoral/research
- Upper undergraduate
- Lower undergraduate
- Basic studies/general academic
- Popular

Some may also include categories for young adult or juvenile works, though these readership levels may be more appropriate for public libraries or K–12 school libraries. Others will have categories for recommended or core titles. Many published books will fall into more than one category and will be assigned multiple readership levels.

Geographic Factors

This parameter can greatly limit the scope of material included in a DDA profile, so it should be considered when a library only wants to collect titles dealing with specific geographic area. This can be as broad as the continent of Africa or as narrow as a specific state or province.

Languages

Most vendors profile titles in more languages than English, though each vendor will have unique offerings. They may also include titles translated from other languages into English.

Formats

Formats can include anything from reference titles to cookbooks, and from travel guides to computer manuals. Librarians should seek feedback from the faculty and researchers in their departments to determine which formats should be included and excluded from DDA. Public librarians should solicit input from their patron base before making decisions on which formats would be best for their DDA plans, while K–12 school librarians should welcome suggestions from their teachers and students.

Editions

Editions will most likely include either newly published content or reprinted content, but some vendors will include parameters for reprints with new material added, supplements, and abridgements. The majority of libraries do not collect reprints unless they have a significant amount of new material, but most DDA plans will include newly published works.

Genres

Many academic and special libraries do not collect genre materials unless special requests are made, but public libraries and some other institutions will want to include genre fiction, poetry, essays, and criticism in their DDA program.

Affiliations

Most vendors now offer the option to add institutional affiliations to profiles, allowing the library to collect everything published by authors who have some connection to their institution or organization. The affiliation can include faculty, alumni, staff, visiting researchers, and students. This is an excellent way to ensure that the various stakeholders of the community are represented in the library's collection.

Other Book Types

There are numerous other nonsubject parameters that should be considered when creating a DDA profile, and not all fall into specific categories. These can include biographies, anthologies, collected works, dissertations and theses, textbooks, and study guides. You should ask your vendor for a full list of nonsubject parameters early in the profile planning stages.

Next Steps

Back Runs and Profile Revision

After the profiling sessions are complete, the vendor representative will create the first iteration of the profile (or profiles) based on the librarian's specifications and his or her own expertise. Most content providers will send a formal agreement or contract listing the specifications of the DDA plan, and this may include a breakdown of the profile parameters. After creating the profile, the collection specialist will generate a back run, also known as a back file title list. The back run will list all titles that matched the parameters of the profile over a specific period of time (usually the past one to three years), had the profile been active during that period. These title lists will include a wealth of bibliographic information for each title, and they should be reviewed carefully by the appropriate subject librarians.

Most back runs will include hundreds or thousands of titles, so a title-by-title analysis is not always the practical approach; in this case, sort by key parameters such as list price, publisher, Library of Congress (LC) class, and readership level. Highlight or otherwise identify titles that seem questionable, and send these back to the vendor. In some cases, the questionable titles will reflect a critical mass that justifies a revision to the profile. In other cases, the questionable titles will not be related and may not warrant a change. Remember that the content generated by a DDA profile does not always equal a purchase and that DDA profiles will inevitably ingest some titles that you may not have handpicked for the collection.

It is not unusual for DDA profiles to go through multiple revisions before generating a back run that is satisfactory and represents the collection goals of the program. This process can take as little as a couple of weeks or as long as several months. Librarians should keep in mind that the profile can continue to be revised after activation.

De-duplication and Record Management

According to the National Information Standards Organization (NISO) survey results on demand-driven acquisition of monographs, duplication control is an acute area of risk and concern for librarians, with some referring to it as a "nightmare" (2013). If working with a single content provider for all collection development, it will be easier to de-duplicate the DDA e-book content against what the library already owns in various formats. When working with multiple vendors and aggregators, duplication checking quickly becomes more complex. Libraries should address the issue of how to handle duplication control with their content provider(s) early in the DDA planning stages to determine what kind of support they can provide and what will need to be managed by the library. Some libraries will collaborate with their vendors to send regular library holdings updates, reducing potential duplication with newly matching DDA titles. Others may decide to handle de-duplication locally and without vendor intervention through the use of spreadsheets or their systems reporting tools. Either way, most libraries working with multiple vendors accept that an inevitable amount of duplication will occur.

Once the DDA profile is activated, the vendor will send an initial file of MARC records to the library. Around the same time, the vendor or aggregator will "switch on" the DDA titles on the e-book platform(s). The library decides how to make DDA records discoverable, whether through the catalog, their local discovery platform, or both. Before the DDA program is up and running, the library should solidify an ongoing schedule of record delivery and removal with their vendor. If the library needs to remove any records from its catalog, the staff members must communicate this to their vendor so the appropriate titles can be "switched off" in their system and on the e-book platform.

Most vendors or aggregators will notify the library when publishers remove titles from DDA programs so they can remove these records from their discovery points. If not, users will be faced with dead links and inaccurate search results. Regardless of the method and schedule for record delivery and removal, a strong communication plan between the library and the vendor/aggregator is vital. Both UNC-CH and NSU experienced challenges with the technical details of loading, modifying, and deleting MARC records, and were thus required to be in close communication with their vendors and aggregators (see the second and third library case studies).

Ongoing Maintenance and Evaluation

Once the MARC records are loaded and the e-book titles are activated, patrons can begin discovering and using DDA content. The work is not over behind the scenes, however, as maintaining and evaluating UDA is an ongoing process. New records will be added for content matching the DDA profile(s) on a regular basis, records will be removed, and the library will receive regular invoices for titles that are loaned or purchased.

It is important for librarians to set up a communication plan not only with their content provider but also among the librarians responsible for any ongoing technical maintenance. At Kent State University Libraries, technical services managers, catalogers, the e-resources librarian, and the acquisitions staff were all involved in various technical processes, necessitating the creation of a technical processes sequence chart (Downey, 2014). Mapping the ongoing processes involved in DDA plans by action, frequency, and persons responsible can prevent confusion and duplicate work, particularly in larger libraries.

Depending on the size and complexity, libraries should plan to evaluate their DDA programs on a recurring basis. Because libraries are often asked by their various stakeholders to provide justification for their collection development practices, they should collect usage data on DDA activity throughout the length of the program. Most libraries rely on their vendor or aggregator for usage statistics, though the quality and types of data reported vary from one aggregator to another. At Rollins College, the librarians "rely on statistics supplied by the vendors for items triggered, items used, turnaways, and funds expended" (see the first library case study). At NSU, "vendor-generated statistics are reviewed multiple times during a given week," and librarians rely on COUNTER statistics to track turnaways (see the second library case study).

Beyond assessing usage on a regular basis, libraries should plan to formally evaluate DDA activity at least once per year. While most libraries choose annual evaluations, biannual or quarterly evaluations can be useful if the DDA plan is new or complex (UF Libraries, 2014, Q12). Formal evaluations should be led by your vendor or aggregator, as they will be able to provide comprehensive analysis of purchasing and usage patterns that may warrant adjustments to profiles, e-book licensing levels, or record management.

Project Planning

As highlighted in chapter 1, "Use-Driven Acquisition Project Management," any DDA plan will benefit from strong project planning. At a basic level, developing and sustaining a DDA plan for e-books will include the elements found in figure 4.1.

Early in the planning stages, the librarian in charge of leading the UDA setup should designate who within the library or department will be responsible for key tasks. The team may involve librarians and staff in collection development, acquisitions, technical services, and e-resources. If you are working with a vendor or aggregator, they may ask for both a main contact and a contact for tech-related issues such as record loading.

The amount of time involved in setting up e-book DDA will vary from library to library. At UNC-CH, it took one full year to begin the DDA program (see the third library case study), while NSU was up and running within three months (see the second library

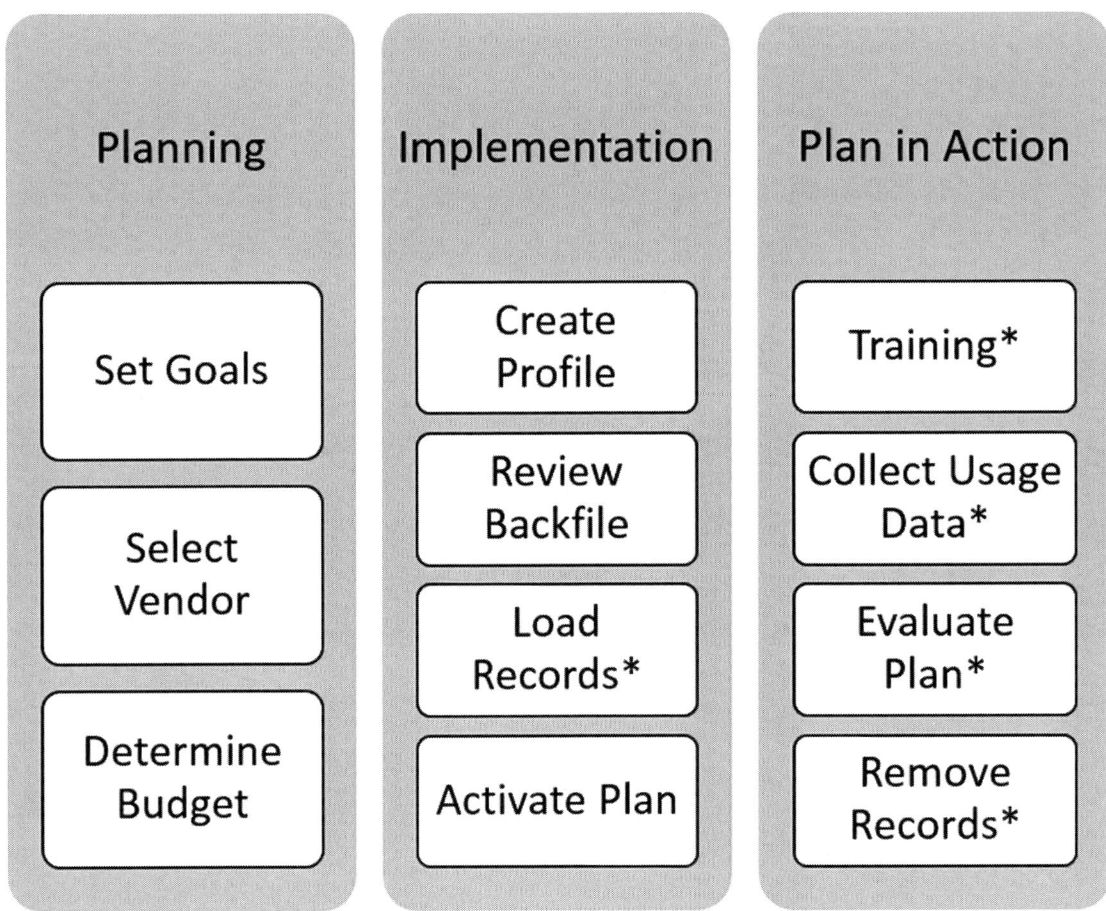

Figure 4.1. Project planning sequence

case study). It is difficult for the team to set solid time lines in the planning process, as internal and external factors will inevitably arise, but you should document the sequence of events (with dates as specific as possible) so you are not forced to reinvent the wheel if new librarians join the team or if you decide to implement DDA again in the future. Once the DDA plan is active, however, it is important to develop solid time lines for ongoing tasks, including which team member is responsible, how often the task occurs, and which action needs to take place.

Key Points

Implementing and maintaining DDA for e-books can be an opportunity for libraries to maximize their book budgets while providing access to a vast universe of titles previously unobtainable to their users. Here are some key points to remember:

- Keep the goals of the plan in mind through all decision-making processes.
- Set realistic time lines and be prepared to make unplanned adjustments.
- Define roles within the library early in the planning stages to determine who will be the "point person" for each task.

- Collaborate with vendors and aggregators to develop the best purchasing models, license levels, profile parameters, MARC records, and usage data that reflect the library's goals.
- Review usage statistics frequently, and plan to collaborate with your vendor on a formal evaluation of the plan at least once per year.

The next chapter will describe how some libraries are collaborating directly with publishers to implement evidence-based acquisition (EBA) plans for e-books and streaming videos.

References

Downey, Kay. 2014. "Technical Services Workflow for Book Jobber-Mediated Demand Driven E-book Acquisitions." *Technical Services Quarterly* 31, no. 1: 1–12. doi:10.1080/07317131.2014.844617.

NISO (National Information Standards Organization). 2013. "Demand Driven Acquisition of Monographs: Summary of Survey Results." http://www.niso.org/.

Nixon, Judith M., Robert S. Freeman, and Suzanne M. Ward. 2011. *Patron-Driven Acquisitions: Current Successes and Future Directions.* New York: Routledge.

University of Florida George A. Smathers Libraries (UF Libraries). 2014. "UDA Library Survey." Last updated August 10, 2015. http://ufdcimages.uflib.ufl.edu/IR/00/00/71/94/00001/UDA_Library_Survey.pdf.

Further Reading

Arndt, Theresa S. 2015. *Getting Started with Demand-Driven Acquisitions for E-books: A LITA Guide.* Chicago: ALA TechSource.

Brooks, Stephen M. 2013. "What's Next for E-book Acquisitions? Challenges for Libraries, Vendors, and Publishers." *Against the Grain* 25, no. 2: 26–28.

Currie, Lea, and Kathy Graves. 2012. "A New Model for Demand-Driven Acquisition." *Kansas Library Association College and University Libraries Section Proceedings* 2:12–16. doi:10.4148/culs.v2i0.1611.

Fischer, Karen S., Michael Wright, Kathleen Clatanoff, Hope Barton, and Edward Shreeves. 2012. "Give 'Em What They Want: A One-Year Study of Unmediated Patron-Driven Acquisition of Ebooks." *College and Research Libraries* 73, no. 5: 469–92.

Goedeken, Edward A., and Karen G. Lawson. 2015. "The Past, Present, and Future of Demand Driven Acquisitions in Academic Libraries." *College and Research Libraries* 76, no. 2 (March): 205–21.

Herrera, Gail. 2012. "Deliver the Ebooks Your Patrons and Selectors Both Want! PDA Program at the University of Mississippi." *Serials Librarian* 63, no. 2: 178–86.

Hodges, Dracine, Cyndi Preston, and Marsha J. Hamilton. "Resolving the Challenge of E-books." *Collection Management* 35, no. 3 (2010): 196–200.

NISO (National Information Standards Organization). 2014. "Demand Driven Acquisition of Monographs: A Recommended Practice of the National Information Standards Organization." June 24. http://www.niso.org/.

ReadersFirst. 2014. "Guide to Library E-book Vendors." 1–17. http://readersfirst.org/.

Library Case Study: Rollins College Library

Reporting: Jonathan Harwell, head of collections and systems
Faculty: 211
Students: 3,153
Type of institution: Private liberal arts
Memberships: Oberlin Group, Center for Research Libraries
Consortia: ICUF (Independent Colleges and Universities of Florida [state]), ACS (Associated Colleges of the South [regional])
Colleges/programs/research centers supported: thirty-nine undergraduate majors; nine master's programs; one executive doctorate in business administration
Materials budget: fiscal year (FY) 2014: $1,046,222.77
Number of UDA plans: two
Current UDA programs: We're incorporating the slip notifications from our approval plan, and shifting our print-approval plan to e-preferred DDA. The approval plan had only covered a few selected subject areas for automatic purchases previously, but we're doing DDA across the board with the exception of art (Library of Congress classification N). We've also begun DDA with streaming video, which is separate from the e-book DDA plan. We're including most subject collections offered for the video plan.
Reasons for incorporating UDA: I implemented DDA at my previous library, and it worked very well. It enabled us to add substantially to our e-book collection, while stretching the budget farther by only paying for the books that were substantially used. I led a college-wide faculty colloquium at my current institution and also talked with the Library Advisory Committee and of course the library faculty. With faculty support, we decided to go forward with DDA for e-books, and around the same time we decided to implement DDA for streaming videos based on a new offer, for the same reason.
Budget model: $30,000 ($20,000 for e-books and $10,000 for streaming video). Approximately 4.7 percent of our yearly collection development budget is used for UDA (excluding endowment funds).
Formats and subjects of UDA program: E-books and streaming video. Previously we only did automatic purchases (approval purchases) in history, Latin American studies, and Walt Whitman studies. We are including virtually all subject areas in our e-book DDA, with the exception of art.
Nonsubject parameters of UDA program: For the e-book plan, we excluded cookbooks (except from Florida), exam guides, form documents, grammar, hymn books, instructor's manuals, lab manuals, music scores, programmed texts, study guides, textbooks, unrevised dissertations, and workbooks; books in print that are in spiral, loose-leaf, or staple bound; books not in English (some included in Spanish); juvenile books; most popular books; most "advanced academic" and "professional" books; facsimile reprints; bibliographies and bio-bibliographies; undersized books; books on local U.S. geography except from our state; and volumes over $100.
Challenges of UDA: Waiting for our distributor (Yankee Book Peddler [YBP]) to get ready to begin our implementation discussion.
Assessment and reporting: We will rely on statistics supplied by the vendors for items triggered, items used, turnaways, and funds expended.

Branding and marketing: We have marketed through articles in our library newsletter and a presentation to our faculty colloquium.

Successful thus far: Yes

Library Case Study: Nova Southeastern University Libraries

Reporting: Andrew Copnick, acquisitions librarian III; Rachel Perry, technical services librarian II

Students: 20,019

Type of institution: Private nonprofit (Library is joint-use funded by Broward County Board of Commissioners.)

Memberships: ACRL (Association of College and Research Libraries)

Consortia: ICUF (Independent Colleges and Universities of Florida), SEFLIN (Southeast Florida Library Information Network)

Colleges/programs/research centers supported: fifty-plus undergraduate colleges and majors (http://www.nova.edu/). Graduate programs in areas such as medicine, law, business, psychology, education, optometry, dentistry, computer sciences, oceanography, pharmacy, and so forth.

Materials budget: FY 2012: $6,521,517. Due to the sensitive nature of funding received from NSU partners, only published financial data from the 2012 ACRL "Academic Library Trends and Statistics" survey have been included.

Number of UDA plans: two

Current UDA programs: The library currently runs two e-book profiles simultaneously—one for the e-book approval plan with slip notifications/approval claims and a separate profile for the MyiLibrary UDA. The two profiles deliver unique content, and there are no duplications (we hope). (1) Coutts/Ingram (UDA: MyiLibrary single-user license). (2) Business Experts Press (UDA: Business Expert Press Digital Library 2010–2014).

Reasons for incorporating UDA: The Alvin Sherman Library initially implemented UDA due to the absence of a subject selector in a key area within collection development. From FY 2013 through the early part of FY 2014, there was no subject librarian selecting items for business and a science, though a new sciences subject librarian started in January 2015. Upon further research, there was realization that a patron-driven acquisition (PDA) could expand the offerings for the user population based on trigger requirements.

Budget model: Approximately 1.87 percent of the yearly collection development budget is used for UDA, or $12,500.

Challenges of UDA: On the administrative end, there has always been a block in terms of creating "deposit accounts" with publishers/vendors. Administration was reluctant to advance funds with no guarantee of continued access by publishers/vendors due to the current state of the publishing/vendor landscape. From the subject librarians, there was little resistance since the allocation for UDA was minimal. However, if the budget allocation was significant vis-à-vis their firm order subject allocations, we are sure that there would have been dissenters to pursuing UDA.

MARC records for the Ebrary PDA were somewhat problematic. Since the publications were foreign imprints, there were diacritics that could not be translated in the III (integrated library system). Of significance, there were MARC records where the 020 (ISBN) was not present at all or had been populated with a subfield "z" (020|z), making the field(s) invalid and nondiscoverable in the public mode or for duplicate checking upon loading. In the end, since there were no alternatives, the records were accepted, and the invalid field was corrected by the e-resources cataloger. The tracking of triggered titles was difficult during the first year of MyiLibrary PDA. MyiLibrary did not set up PDA-specific accounts or "purchased/nonpurchased" collections. Instead, once an e-book was triggered from the "nonpurchased" collection, it was moved to the Alvin Sherman Library's e-book firm order account for invoicing. Needless to say, if one was not logging into the MyiLibrary administration (usage collection) site on a daily basis (or even more than that), a title could be triggered and shifted for invoicing the same day. Without any reporting structure by MyiLibrary, there were instances where a triggered title was not captured and was "lost" for budgetary tracking until the invoice appeared. This was addressed to sales support staff in an August 2014 meeting. Consequently, a PDA-specific account was created and two distinct collections were formatted for accurate tracking (nonpurchased collection *and* purchased collection). At the beginning of a given fiscal year, the library submits a purchase order for the maximum dollar appropriation. Due to reporting issues (e.g., triggers) and the account setup, Coutts went over the allotted budget by approximately $1,200. The reporting structure has been improved greatly for the current fiscal year (FY 2015), and we do not anticipate any similar issues.

Assessment and reporting: Vendor-generated statistics are reviewed multiple times during a given week in order to prevent any titles slipping through the cracks and not being reflected in budget documents. We look carefully at the number of titles that have not reached their trigger point to prove the success of the UDA plan in terms of free accesses to content. The statistics that are viewed tend to be on a broader time period than the current fiscal year's PDA since there are titles that have carried over from the previous fiscal year. Both collection development and acquisitions view the COUNTER statistics for turnaways since the MyiLibrary license is for single user only (SUPO). Statistics viewed by acquisitions are largely those that pertain to tracking the trigger of a title to prevent an expenditure in excess of the budgetary allocation, instead of the performance of the e-book and its contents, which largely rests in collection development's responsibility. The COUNTER statistics for business experts will be used to determine the usage for the e-books from 2010 to 2014 since it is a UDA-based program for their e-book collections.

Record management: The general policy in technical services is to simply suppress the bibliographic record if the e-book title is not being further considered as part of the PDA. This way, the user cannot discover the title (and link) to the e-book and thus cannot trigger a purchase. At the same time, acquisitions informs the vendor to discontinue access via its e-book platform (e.g., when the vendor makes a grievous error and activates a publisher that is clearly listed on the NSPs to exclude). By suppressing the record, technical services (acquisitions and cataloging) can still have the bibliographic record for statistical gathering.

Branding and marketing: We do not market our UDA program.

Success of the program: Our UDAs have been successful in terms of service for dollars spent. Our first UDA plan (Ebrary) increased our access to e-books by over $38,000 and spent only $7,200. Our second UDA plan (MyiLibrary) increased our catalog access value by $73,889 and spent only $11,644. We have not yet designed an evaluation instrument to determine whether the PDA is successful in terms of collection development (i.e., are subject area voids caused by PDA?) or benefit to patrons (i.e., do the titles patrons select fill collection development gaps?).

Library Case Study: University of North Carolina at Chapel Hill Libraries

Reporting: Luke Swindler, collections management officer
Faculty: 3,969
Students: 29,127
Type of institution: Public
Memberships: ARL (Association of Research Libraries; library) and AAU (Association of American Universities; university)
Consortia: TRLN (Triangle Research Libraries Network); Carolina Consortium; ASERL (Association of Southeastern Research Libraries); NERL (NorthEast Research Libraries)/CRL (Center for Research Libraries)
Colleges/programs/research centers supported: 74 doctoral, 107 master's, and 71 bachelor's programs covering nearly the entire academic disciplinary spectrum
Materials budget: projected circa $15 million for FY 2014/2015
Number of UDA plans: one (Ebook Library [EBL] via YBP)
Current UDA programs: UNC's UDA is integrated into its overall schema for acquiring/leasing English-language monographs generally and a hierarchical mosaic for e-book acquisitions specifically rather than a stand-alone program. The major elements of UNC's comprehensive monographic acquisitions program include the following: extensive as well as specialized/targeted approval plans, covering both print and e-preferred; standing orders for publishers and series; over two dozen subject librarians generating firm orders; acquisitions of publishers' entire e-book output; purchasing e-books packages by publisher and subject; leased current e-books collections, ranging from specialized, such as Safari Tech Books, to comprehensive, such as Ebrary's Academic Complete; and large retrospective e-books archive acquisitions covering all titles available, for example, Oxford University Press and Sage. UNC's UDA is campus wide, covering all relevant subjects and encompassing its separately administered health sciences and law libraries as well as the main system. Consequently, the initial pool included over $1 million in e-books at list price, with a large retrospective file to be added in 2015.
Reasons for incorporating UDA: Strategically, UDA is part of a two-year, systematic-staged plan to selectively shift appropriate monographic English-language acquisitions to e-books; this was done to improve support for instruction and research by increasing the number of monographs available to faculty and students. UNC campus libraries implemented a DDA e-books program in order to achieve the following goals:

- improve support for the academic enterprise by presenting faculty and students with a large number of potentially useful and relevant e-books for possible acquisition, with the aggregate number and cost of titles in the DDA program being well beyond what campus libraries could ever afford to buy;
- align monographic acquisitions more closely with active instructional and research needs **A**utomatically, **A**lgorithmically, and **A**t point of need in real time;

- target collections dollars to meet actual needs based on patron use;
- get a better and broad-based sense of the patrons' acceptance of e-books and their willingness to use them; and
- save subject librarians' time selecting and technical services staff's time processing monographs, especially for publishers where few titles are automatically shipped and/or selected.

Reducing monographic expenditures per se is *not* an objective; rather, UNC libraries want to ensure that titles acquired under this program meet actual user needs. At the same time, costs will be carefully monitored on a weekly basis initially and on a monthly basis after the program is in place so they will not significantly exceed what is currently being spent on monographic acquisitions (including approval auto-shipments and firm orders from the publishers included in the DDA plan). Within the above context, UNC's overall goals for DDA are as follows:

- Ultimate goal: increase/improve/support the academic enterprise, including both instruction and research
- Broad goal: enhance the collections' evolution to a 24/7 virtual service
- Specific goal: provide faculty and students with a large number of potentially useful and relevant e-books beyond what campus libraries could ever afford to buy

Budget model: Integrated into a circa $1.5 million combined monographic approval plans accounts with YBP library services. Because UNC's UDA with EBL is via YBP library services, it has no specific budget behind it. Consequently, funding the UDA plan will come from shifting dollars from the YBP approval and firm order accounts—a strategy that underscores its integration within the larger book acquisitions matrix.

Content level and subjects of UDA plan: Only e-books, with a print component scheduled to be added in early 2016. The UDA profile specifies that only titles with a list price under $250 will automatically populate the pool; used YBP audience and content nonsubject parameters to exclude popular titles and low-level textbooks; reprints excluded; some presses excluded if not appropriate or if UNC is buying their e-books via entire packages; and university presses excluded until early 2015. Although both borrowing charges and auto-purchases have been low, in 2015 UNC will institute mediated acquisition the first time a reader exceeds the five-minute free browse purchase when the short-term lending (STL) charge exceeds $50. In such cases, the patron is presented with a "Request Library Purchase" button to click if he or she wants to continue reading the UDA e-book. As a rule, the library will approve automatic purchase of these titles ASAP, which triggers the patron receiving an e-mail indicating that the e-book is available with a link to click for accessing it.

Challenges of UDA: UNC did a great deal of planning and therefore had no internal disagreements. On the other hand, we spent a great deal of time working out the technical details with both EBL and YBP on such issues as entering MARC records into the online catalog and handling deletions from the DDA poll.

Assessment and reporting: No system in place yet. Will rely on EBL for usage data. No decisions yet made on what kinds of statistics to collect other than monitoring specific titles registering usage and expenditures on short-term loans and auto-purchases.

Record management: The only deletions have been from EBL when the publisher withdrew a title. On the other hand, UNC selectors *may* firm order a title in the UDA plan at any time and for any reason, and they are encouraged to do so when they notice an e-book in the UDA plan has registered a costly short-term loan (STL) charge and they expect additional use.

Branding and marketing: Made no special efforts to publicize UDA to users.

Successful thus far: Yes.

CHAPTER 5

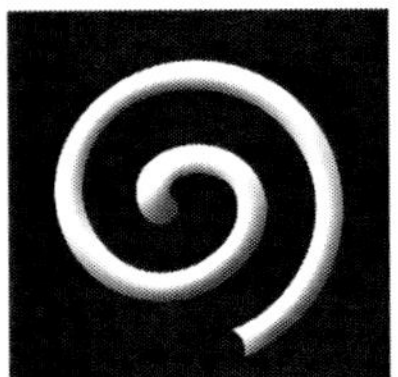

Evidence-Based Acquisitions (EBA)

IN THIS CHAPTER

- ▷ Choosing publishers and content
- ▷ Developing and implementing an EBA plan
- ▷ Partnering with consortia
- ▷ Assessing the EBA plan

EVIDENCE-BASED ACQUISITIONS (EBA) is a relatively new model for acquiring access to and ownership of content in libraries. EBA can also be referred to as evidence-based selection (EBS). According to the National Information Standards Organization's (NISO) "Demand Driven Acquisition of Monographs: A Recommended Practice," "Evidence-based acquisition . . . is triggered by reaching the end of an agreed upon time period and spending a pre-negotiated amount of money, making title selections based on the evidence of usage gathered during the trial access period" (NISO, 2014, 10). EBA provides a variation on traditional demand-driven acquisition plans for e-books (see chapter 4, "Demand-Driven Acquisitions [DDA]"), allowing for more mediation in selection and controlled spending. EBA plans are used by libraries to acquire e-books and streaming video, though other formats are being explored by content providers.

This chapter will focus on developing, implementing, and assessing EBA plans. It begins with an overview of selection models and content providers and includes factors to consider when implementing EBA. You will find useful tips for managing and assessing EBA plans. The chapter presents a case study example of how one academic library approached this model successfully, as well as an interview with an e-book vendor who partners with libraries to incorporate EBA plans into their collection development strategies.

REASONS LIBRARIES SHOULD IMPLEMENT EBA PLANS

- ✓ MARC records can be conveniently batch loaded to simplify setup.
- ✓ EBA plans require little maintenance and management once in operation.
- ✓ Libraries can offer access to a wealth of content while paying for a fraction of the value during a set time period.
- ✓ EBA plans can be an efficient and intelligent way to spend use-driven acquisition (UDA) funds on publisher content that librarians already know is valued and sought after by their users.
- ✓ Publisher e-book collections and streaming video collections are available by subject area or discipline and can often be tailored title by title.
- ✓ No digital rights management means fewer restrictions for users.
- ✓ Librarians can decide what gets purchased with deposit funds and how to decide on purchasing factors, whether usage based or otherwise.
- ✓ All or a portion of a publisher's content is made available for EBA plans, including backlist titles often at reduced prices.
- ✓ EBA plans strike a satisfactory balance between user-driven acquisition and librarian-mediated final purchasing decisions.
- ✓ Acquiring content from one publisher offers a consistent and high-level experience for users.

Selection Models and Content Providers

EBA is attractive for many reasons, but a significant reason is that it allows librarians more control over the selection of purchased titles than does a traditional demand-driven acquisition (DDA) plan. Subject selectors are informed by usage data collected during the EBA plan period, but they can exercise their expertise when making ultimate purchasing decisions. In the access versus ownership debate, EBA plans strike a happy balance between providing access to a wide universe of content and purchasing only a subset of that content that shows high usage or institutional value.

In chapter 4 you read how DDA e-book plans have expanded and how content providers have evolved to offer endless combinations of licensing, purchasing, and selecting models that can be adapted by libraries of all shapes and sizes. Perhaps because it is a relatively new model for acquisition, EBA content providers offer fewer options. Libraries can benefit from out-of-the-box collections and processes that require less staff time to set up and manage. If the diversification of traditional DDA e-book plans is any indication, content providers will likely be open to collaboration that explores the potential for local customization of EBA plans.

Few content providers or publishers offer EBA, with only a handful of e-book publishers and streaming-video services occupying the EBA market. These formats make sense for EBA, as use of digital content among library patrons is on the rise and demand for cost-effective acquisition options is high. Not all publishers offer EBA as a purchasing option, primarily because a certain infrastructure must be in place in order for the plans to function: a platform for viewing and managing content; the ability to provide comprehensive usage reports; and the staffing needed to manage the plans for multiple libraries.

Table 5.1. List of EBA content providers

VENDOR/PUBLISHER	MORE INFORMATION	CURRENT EBA PROVIDER?
Cambridge University Press	"For Librarians: Evidence Based Acquisition," http://ebooks.cambridge.org/	Yes
Alexander Street Press	"Evidence-Based Acquisition for Streaming Video," http://alexanderstreet.com/	Yes
Elsevier	Contact your Elsevier sales representative to learn more.	Yes
Gale	"Gale Launches Innovative Purchase Model for E-books," http://news.cengage.com/	Yes, for reference
Wiley	"E-books," http://www.wiley.com/	Yes
Sage	Contact your Sage sales representative to learn more.	Yes
Taylor & Francis	Contact your Taylor & Francis sales representative to learn more.	Yes
Rittenhouse	Contact your Rittenhouse sales representative to learn more.	Yes

Most libraries operating DDA plans choose e-books (UF Libraries, 2014, Q7) as their format of choice, but streaming video promises to be a burgeoning format for EBA plans. Table 5.1 provides an overview of the current content providers who offer EBA plans. Models and products change at a rapid pace, so contact your vendor or publisher representative for up-to-date details.

Developing the EBA Plan

Setting Goals and Budgets

Lisa Nachtigall, director of sales development for digital books with Wiley, states, "EBA can be an effective complement to a core collection, and how the library decides to implement that can be based on budgets and collection goals" (see the vendor spotlight). As should be the case when considering any new acquisitions strategy, it is vital for libraries to set goals early in the planning stages and shape decisions based on those goals. Chapter 2's "Five Questions Regarding Collection Strategies" (page 15) will be helpful to address when determining if or how to incorporate UDA methods into collection building, but librarians may also want to ask the following questions when considering EBA:

1. Is the library's primary goal access, ownership, or a combination of both?
2. Does the library's primary goal include a greater return on investment (ROI) for purchased e-books and/or streaming videos?
3. Do the librarians prefer unmediated UDA models or some mediation in purchasing decisions?
4. Are current e-book subscription packages providing value to users through repeat use, justifying annual expenditures?
5. Are librarian-selected individual e-book titles seeing enough usage to justify their purchase?
6. Are there specific publishers whose content is highly valued and consistently used?

Goals also depend on the format used for EBA plans. Libraries may consider EBA plans for streaming videos if their goals include phasing out obsolete technologies or the ability to manipulate video content by creating playlists and clips and embedding into course management systems. Both e-books and streaming videos free up precious shelf space and provide effective access to content for distance learners or users who may not frequent the library physically. EBA plans for e-books and streaming video work to complement other traditional methods of collection building, such as approval plans and firm ordering, but will most likely not replace other methods entirely.

Budgets play a major role in all collection-building decisions. At the heart of each new strategy is the desire to maximize spending on content patrons will use, preferably over and over again, for as long as possible. The University of Liverpool library experienced periods of budget growth and reduction from year to year as their users began to demand more e-books; they saw success with subscription packages from aggregators and publishers, and tried to fill in the gaps with single e-book purchases. After analyzing their various collection development strategies, they embarked on three EBA trials in order to fulfill their goals of providing users with access to expansive collections while deciding which ones they should purchase annually, thus focusing budgets on content with evidence of use (Bucknell, 2012).

Once librarians have decided that EBA plans fit their goals, they must decide on an amount to deposit with their chosen content provider(s). NISO's "Demand Driven Acquisition of Monographs: A Recommended Practice" suggests, "Often used as a starting point in negotiations is to base it on recent annual spending on monographs from that publisher" (NISO, 2014, 10). This way, the library is not faced with increased costs from previous years and the publisher is still guaranteed a minimum spend from the library. Though recent annual spending can be a good starting point for determining the deposit amount, publishers will consider other factors such as the number of titles included in the plan, whether newly published titles will be added throughout the course of the plan, expected usage, the size of the institution, and so forth. Some content providers require minimum deposit amounts, so begin negotiations early in the planning process.

If sustainability is part of the library's goal in implementing EBA plans, then the library will need to develop an ongoing model for funding from year to year. This might include setting aside monograph or video funds with the intent of being used for EBA plan deposits, though most libraries experience unpredictable funding from one year to the next. Some libraries, such as Brigham Young University (BYU), sustain their EBA plans by determining which subject areas the purchased e-books align with and then pulling funds from these appropriate areas. This has proved to be an ongoing challenge for BYU's subject selectors, and they cite sustainable funding as "perhaps the biggest challenge in implementing EBA" (see the library case study).

Choosing Content

Once goals and budgets are set, it is time to decide which content to include in the EBA plan. Options will differ from publisher to publisher, but most EBA e-book plans are grouped into subject collections. Librarians should choose subject collections that support the goals of their plan and that fit their budgets. Some libraries look to their current collection development parameters to inform their EBA plans. At BYU, librarians wanted the parameters of their EBA plans to mirror their existing approval plans as closely as possible (see the library case study). EBA streaming-video plans offer collections by subject or by distributor (see chapter 9, "Streaming Video").

Unlike traditional DDA e-book plans, profiling the EBA plan involves little more than deciding on content providers, subjects, publication dates, and deposit amount. Most publishers offer scholarly e-book collections but may extend options to add textbooks and reference works to the EBA plan. Some publishers allow libraries to create bespoke collections tailored to institutional needs. As with most UDA models, publishers may withhold some content (usually front-list or high-demand titles) from EBA plans to maintain revenue from individual title sales. It's important to remember that EBA plan content is hosted on individual publisher platforms, so functionality of and user satisfaction with these platforms should be weighed when considering multiple EBA plans. Will your users be confused or frustrated by navigating multiple e-book or streaming-video platforms? Another point of consideration is how long the EBA plan will run. Most publishers allow for a six- or twelve-month access period, but twelve months is recommended in order to a get a holistic view of usage over an entire year. For some content providers, the more funds a library commits in their deposit, the longer the access period.

Managing Technical Details

Users must be able to discover and access EBA content in order to drive the usage that will inform purchasing decisions. Depending on the technical setup at the library, be sure to take advantage of the (usually) free MARC records provided by publishers; these should be loaded into the library catalog to facilitate discovery. If the library uses a discovery service as well as, or instead of, a catalog, the appropriate titles or collections should be activated, though library staff may need to work with publishers and a discovery service provider to make sure the correct collections are available. At BYU, "All bibliographic records associated with EBA titles are loaded into our discovery tool and online catalog database in order to provide discovery and access" (library case study).

An important consideration is whether or not newly published content will be added to the EBA plan throughout the access period. If so, work with your content provider to solidify a schedule for how often new MARC records will be reviewed. Formulate a schedule within the appropriate library department for loading these records on an ongoing basis. Librarians should develop a plan for how to handle records for unpurchased content at the end of the access period. If the EBA plan continues for another year, leave the records as they are and allow for further discovery and use. If the EBA plan will not be ongoing, the records should be removed or suppressed, and any associated collections deactivated in your discovery service.

Librarians should also discuss de-duplication with their EBA publishers early in the planning process. Some libraries have the personnel and resources to handle de-duplication in their own departments, but others will need to solicit the expertise of their content providers. If the library has approval plans running that may include content from EBA plan publishers, coordinate with the approval plan vendors to ensure that specific collections, subject areas, or entire publishers are excluded from the UDA plans.

Consortia EBA Plans

Most EBA plans are developed for individual libraries, but there are cases where libraries collaborate on a shared plan. One such plan started as a pilot in 2014 by the libraries at Florida State University (FSU) and the University of Florida (UF). The two libraries have partnered with Cambridge University Press and access the same e-book content from this publisher. Cambridge adds records to the plan on an ongoing basis so users from both libraries have access to a larger number of e-book titles.

There are benefits for the libraries and Cambridge University Press for conducting a shared EBA. The libraries receive a discount on the e-books purchased, and users have access to hundreds of e-books; the selection process is separate for each institution and allows each library the opportunity to select e-books for purchase that are most suitable for their institutional collections. The FSU/UF shared plan is similar to the "buyer's club" purchasing model. From the publisher's perspective, this shared e-books plan is beneficial because usage statistics may show high use beyond the titles purchased, urging the libraries to make additional purchases. Also, the publisher believes the final outcomes will be advantageous and the libraries will continue the EBA plan annually (Gallagher, 2014).

The same aspects of EBA that appeal to individual libraries are true for consortia as well, including fewer DRM restrictions and separate platforms, and simple deposit accounting. EBA plans have less technical overhead than traditional DDA e-book plans, as record loading is simplified and e-books are purchased in batches. For library groups and consortia, de-duplication is somewhat easier; content from a publisher, especially based on imprint years, can be blocked from other approval and UDA plans.

Assessment and Sustainability

At the end of the predetermined access period, librarians will be faced with the task of analyzing usage data and deciding which titles to purchase. Librarians should ask their EBA content providers the following questions in order to plan for assessment:

- What kind of data will they provide during and at the end of the access period? Can librarians access this data themselves throughout the access period?
- What is the turnaround time for deciding on purchases? Most publishers allow for thirty days but may be willing to negotiate for longer.
- What if the dollar amount of the content used does not equal the amount of the deposit? Can funds be rolled over?

Depending on the answers, librarians should plan for how to handle the assessment period before it arrives. If there is a set turnaround time for deciding on purchases, make sure it falls during a time when the main decision makers will be available. Some content providers do not allow for librarian mediation in purchasing decisions; instead, titles with the highest use during the access period will be automatically deducted from the deposit amount. This works well for libraries that don't have the time or resources to devote to title-by-title selection, but librarians must be comfortable with relinquishing that control.

Individual content providers will differ, but most will offer standard COUNTER usage statistics that include

- usage by subject area;
- usage by publisher-determined subject collection;
- overall usage by title;
- title-by-title usage from most used to least used;
- top search terms;

- number of visits to EBA content provider platform; and
- number of unique devices used to access EBA content provider platform.

It is vital to develop criteria for how content will be selected for purchase at the end of the access period. Some libraries will choose the titles with the highest use regardless of subject area. Others involve selectors from all subjects included with the intent of scattering purchases across multiple subject areas. Lisa Nachtigall suggests that the latter option may be a way to solicit funding for EBA programs from multiple subject budgets (see the vendor spotlight). Librarians should keep their original goals in mind when making selection decisions but should also be open to new ways of interpreting the data.

Libraries should develop a sustainable, long-term plan for incorporating it into ongoing collection-building strategies. Traditional DDA e-book plans can inform EBA endeavors, such as identifying which publisher's content is being consistently purchased or loaned through DDA. This publisher may be a good candidate for a targeted EBA plan. Some librarians, such as Gayle Chan of the University of Hong Kong Libraries, compared usage of EBA collections to usage of an aggregator e-book collection, determining that the EBA collections provide greater value (2012). Others, such as BYU, have developed a sustainable model for funding their EBA plans that involves contributions from a variety of subject areas, allowing individual subject selectors to be stakeholders in the success of the plans (see the library case study).

Key Points

Many libraries find themselves deliberating the access versus ownership question: is it more important to provide users with immediate access to a variety of materials or for the library to own those materials in perpetuity? Instead of forcing librarians to choose one over the other, EBA plans allow for a bit of both. Here are some key points to remember:

- Keep the goals of the plan in mind through all decision-making processes.
- For best results, involve subject selectors in the planning and assessment stages.
- Collaborate with content providers to create EBA collections that best fit your goals and budget.
- Develop criteria for selecting purchases, but allow for some flexibility based on usage statistics.
- Consider consortia EBA as a way to stretch budgets even further.
- Employ EBA as a complement to other collection-building methods such as DDA, approval plans, and title-by-title firm ordering.

The next chapter will explore how some libraries implement UDA models through consortia.

References

Bucknell, Terry. 2012. "Buying by the Bucketful: A Comparative Study of E-book Acquisition Strategies." *Insights: The UKSG journal* 25, no. 1: 51–60. doi:10.1629/2048-7754.25.1.51.

Chan, Gayle. 2012. "A Sustainable E-book Purchase Model: A Successful Partnership." *Library Connect Newsletter: Evolving Collections and Services* 10, no. 2: 5.

Gallagher, Don. 2014. E-mail to authors. August 19.
NISO (National Information Standards Organization). 2014. "Demand Driven Acquisition of Monographs: A Recommended Practice of the National Information Standards Organization." June 24. http://www.niso.org/.
University of Florida George A. Smathers Libraries (UF Libraries). 2014. "UDA Library Survey." Last updated August 10, 2015. http://ufdcimages.uflib.ufl.edu/IR/00/00/71/94/00001/UDA_Library_Survey.pdf.

Further Reading

Alderson, Carolyn. 2014. "Evidence Provides More Options for E-book Acquisition." *Research Information*, April 7. http://www.researchinformation.info/.
"George Mason Joins Alexander Street's EBA Pilot Program." 2014. *Advanced Technology Libraries* 43, no. 1: 3.

Library Case Study: Brigham Young University Library

Reporting: Robert G. Murdoch, associate university librarian for collection development and technical services
Number of full-time faculty: 1,500
Number of full-time students: 30,000
Type of institution: Private
Memberships: Association of Research Libraries, Center for Research Libraries, Scholarly Publishing and Academic Resources Coalition (SPARC), LYRASIS, Digital Library Federation
Consortia: Utah Academic Library Consortium (UALC), Greater Western Library Alliance (GWLA)
Colleges/degree programs/research centers supported: Twelve separate colleges, each support both undergraduate and graduate programs
Library materials budget: fiscal year 2014–2015: $10,574,195
Number of evidence-based plans: At the present time we operate two evidence-based plans.
Budget allocation for evidence-based plans: $130,000.00
Current EBA programs: BYU has made the decision to incorporate evidence-based acquisition models into its overall collection development strategies and directions. The selection of the EBA programs is based on the quality of the content and subject/discipline coverage. We want the content covered in the EBA programs to match as closely as possible the selection profiles created and maintained by our various subject librarians for their approval plans. We attempt to involve subject librarians in the processes of establishing EBA initiatives/programs and assessing EBA programs. A number of usage and subject area metrics reports are shared regularly with subject librarians to be used in monitoring trends and collection development assessment and planning. Each individual EBA program has a set overall dollar commitment for the defined EBA cycle (in our case, a twelve-month period). At the conclusion of an EBA cycle, subject librarians review the usage activity and other criteria and make decisions as to which titles to purchase within the set EBA budget. Once titles to be purchased have been identified, the purchase price is charged against a subject librar-

ian's collections development account, based on the subject of the selected book. All bibliographic records associated with EBA titles are loaded into our discovery tool and online catalog database in order to provide discovery and access. EBA titles that are not purchased remain in our discovery layers.

Reasons for incorporating EBA: Based on our library's early experiences and assessments, we determined EBA had a number of benefits and decided to add EBA to our collection development tool set. We looked for EBA partnerships with publishers/vendors whose content best matched our university's curriculum, research agenda, and profile and who provide useful and regular metrics and budget/expense reports. We like our EBA programs because they provide our users unlimited access to the entire suite of titles associated with the program; the dollar commitment for the EBA program is defined up front, which is easy to budget and manage; EBA eliminates expenditure surprises; and EBA offers flexibility in setting purchase criteria.

Length of EBA plans: The length of time necessary to define and activate our EBA programs varied with each publisher. Most of the difference in activation time revolved around initial negotiations relating to issues such as follows: (1) the scope of the content included in the EBA model; (2) the price guarantee for the EBA cycle; (3) factors impacting the content to be included or excluded (encyclopedias, price, sets, continuations, etc.); and (4) reports, metrics, and data. One EBA program took approximately four months to set up. Another EBA program took well over a year to negotiate what the EBA program would look like and another two months to implement.

Formats and subjects of EBA plans: We currently have two active EBA programs for e-books. Last year we also had an EBA program for streaming video. Both of our current EBA programs focus primarily on the following:

- sciences
- engineering
- technology
- medicine/health sciences
- social sciences

Nonsubject parameters connected to our EBA programs include the following:

- price
- publisher
- publication date
- sets, encyclopedias, continuations

Budget model: Approximately 1 percent of the collection development budget is connected to EBA.

Support from stakeholders: There has been no resistance from the administration in implementing EBA. They see the benefit of purchasing those materials having an active usage profile. Having an acquisition model that purchases materials on a just-in-time mindset rather than just in case was an easy sale. There has been some resistance from subject librarians to implementing EBA, mostly from librarians in the humanities disciplines. For the most part, subject librarians with collection responsibilities in science, technology, business, and social science expressed little concern with EBA. Concerns include the following:

- increased opportunity to mismanage a comprehensive collection development program (create "holes" in collection areas);
- loss of control of collection development and expenditure decisions;
- reluctance to draw EBA expenditures from subject librarian collection development accounts;
- not wanting to use subject librarian funds to purchase EBA selections; and
- fear that EBA will lead to the demise of the subject librarian collection development role.

Challenges of EBA: The development of a sustainable funding model was perhaps the biggest challenge in implementing EBA. Once we determined we wanted EBA to be an ongoing element in our collection development program, we needed a way to fund the program from one year to the next. In order to fund EBA, each subject librarian knows in advance that EBA expenditures will be applied against collection accounts that most closely match the subject area of the title being purchased. This means a portion of a subject librarian's collections account needs to be held back until the end of the EBA cycle. If not all funds are needed, the subject librarian is able to carry them forward to the new budget year. If not enough funds were set aside for EBA expenditures, then the deficit balance is taken from the next year's budget appropriation. Getting the desired level of library faculty and staff support for EBA was somewhat of a challenge in the beginning and remains a challenge for a handful of subject librarians.

Assessment and reporting: The primary source for EBA collection data is the publisher associated with the EBA program. Data includes the following:

- title usage by subject area
- title usage by publisher's subject collection areas
- overall usage report by title
- report for ranking title usage by most used to least used
- usage report showing the number of visits and number of unique devices used to access EBA site per month throughout the year (also compares one year against the next)

Marketing: We have not done a great deal of marketing for our EBA programs. We have had subject librarians add information on their subject guides about the content available from our EBA publishers.

Successful thus far: To date we are judging EBA to be a significant success and benefit to our students and faculty. The overall usage of EBA content is meeting or exceeding expectation. Usage of the materials is broad based, covering many disciplines. We are spending collection development funds only on materials being used. The quality and timeliness of the resources being purchased is very good.

Vendor Spotlight: Wiley

Interview with: Lisa Nachtigall, director of sales development for digital books

Why do you think publishers and e-book providers are offering a model like EBA? I think what we're seeing is the pendulum between access and ownership swinging in such a way that it is very difficult for us to keep up with changing approaches to collection development. Budgets are under incredible pressure as the delivery of scholarship meets new developments in technology. So, in some ways, these new models were created to add more buying power to every dollar spent. The evidence-based programs developed by Wiley and other publishers became a response to the adoption of short-term loans (STL) as a default acquisition model for many libraries. These publisher programs have been a way for us to maintain a direct relationship with librarians who were looking for a new way of purchasing e-books. A key element of that direct relationship is that we can help libraries get the most out of the content they are buying. Our editors and our marketers can help drive awareness of the quality of the scholarship and of the authors who publish with Wiley. We consider it part of our role as the publisher to help the library respond to the "ROI question," and we can do that most effectively in a direct conversation with librarians.

What formats do you offer for EBA? We offer it for e-books on Wiley Online Library and have started to discuss what an offer for reference works might look like.

Do you require a minimum deposit to start an EBA plan? Yes. We have three tiers based on full-time enrollment (FTE), and there is a deposit account that initiates the program.

What are some of the challenges of implementing EBA plans from the vendor perspective? We need to put more effort into providing usage statistics that help tell the story to the librarian. At a most basic level, the librarian can look at the usage data and buy the top titles based on that usage. But what we've also seen is that there can be benefits to looking at the data in other ways, like looking at usage by subject, where librarians are able to see usage in certain subjects where they might not have anticipated seeing usage or where they might not have been purchasing in digital format. This can help get funding for an EBA program from multiple subject budgets.

What kinds of usage data do you provide to customers at the end of their use period? The standard COUNTER reports are available, but we take those reports and reformat the information, and provide additional information on top-used titles, top-used subjects, search terms, and so forth. Basic usage reports are available as often as libraries want to use them, and the dashboard reports are available after nine months, and then again at the end of the twelve-month period to aid in selection.

Are there situations in which you would not recommend EBA? I have a global view of our digital book sales, and what we've seen with some of our library partners is that a library might not have the resources (time or staff) to analyze and interpret usage by digging into those reports. Or sometimes, a library is primarily interested in building their digital holdings through large collection purchases without the input of user activity. Again, it goes to the continuum between access and ownership. The real beauty of an evidence-based model is that the librarians still have the control over what gets purchased. But I wouldn't recommend these more nuanced models if librarians are primarily concerned about buying only what they already know they need for classroom support. When I sat on the NISO committee to develop DDA recommendations, a key recommendation we made was to be clear about your goals and objectives when selecting a new acquisition model. If you do that, you'll have a model that works for you.

Do you consider EBA to be a successful acquisitions model? I think that's for the librarians to answer. From our perspective, it has allowed us to work directly with customers who might not have been prepared to make a firm purchasing commitment up front before having that evidence of usage. It's been successful as a sales model because we have seen libraries come in for a second year and now a third year. EBA can be an effective complement to a core collection, and how the library decides to implement that can be based on budgets and collection goals.

Where do you see EBA plans moving in the next five years? We are starting to have discussions about introducing it for other types of content. There are so many new models for e-book acquisition starting to bubble up to the surface, and one thing that we've learned over the last few years is that it's critical to talk more with librarians about what their needs are before we come up with new models. And models need to change. One of the things we've started to do with our own model is to slice it in different ways. The conversations help these models evolve: which models do you use to learn, which models do you use to move forward, and frankly, which help you achieve your goals? We've had customers who have seen how much money they're spending on individual publisher content through STL, for instance, and realized that the spending isn't resulting in ownership because of how triggers are set. And their goal is ownership! Knowing this about the library's experience is such a critical part of the direct conversation between publishers and librarians. Introducing models like EBA has given us a way to restore those conversations that had been going through third parties for the last few years. My colleagues and I can work with a librarian to help drive discoverability and usage of Wiley content on the Wiley platform in a way that an aggregated e-book provider does not. It's really about the goals and objectives in your program, and if driving usage is a key component of your return on investment analysis, then that's something we can help you do.

CHAPTER 6

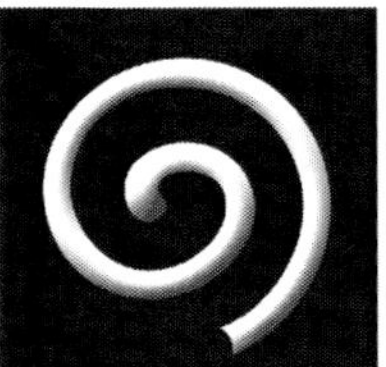

Shared and Consortia Plans

IN THIS CHAPTER

- ▷ Determining goals for collections and budgets
- ▷ Reviewing DDA models for consortia
- ▷ Selecting and collaborating with vendors and publishers
- ▷ Modifying the DDA plan as needed

THIS CHAPTER OFFERS LIBRARIANS PRACTICAL information and fundamental points to consider in the design, implementation, and management phases of a shared use-driven acquisition (UDA) plan to acquire e-books, as well as a library case study. For libraries interested in participating in shared plans, two UDA methods are available for the acquisition of e-books: (1) what is now the standard UDA model in the library world, the demand-driven acquisition (DDA) model, also referred to as the patron-driven acquisition (PDA) model; and (2) the evidence-based acquisition method (EBA). The DDA model is by far the more prevalent model for consortia e-book plans, although the EBA method has the potential to gain ground. Shared e-book plans are typically developed by libraries working with their consortium, but there are many examples of libraries partnering outside consortia.

Background

There are several challenges when developing a shared UDA plan. The main objective is to create a plan with appropriate e-book content that generates substantial usage across all participating libraries. Another challenge is that the plan must be affordable and have an allocation system that is fair and equitable for all members of the group. Shared plans are inherently complicated as they require the libraries within a group to communicate

REASONS TO LAUNCH SHARED E-BOOK UDA PLANS

- ✓ Shared e-book plans provide initiatives for a consortium to build on collective collections that can also benefit individual library holdings.
- ✓ Shared e-book plans allow library consortia to pool funds and utilize collection budgets in creative ways.
- ✓ Many e-books will be accessible to library users, whether they are purchased or not.
- ✓ Libraries in a consortium with smaller full-time enrollment (FTE) or restrictive budgets will benefit from access to content that would never have been made available otherwise.
- ✓ E-books will get repeated (even heavy) use across many libraries.
- ✓ Shared plans can provide centralized budgeting, record loading, and other workflow efficiencies.
- ✓ Usage statistics and comparison reports (e.g., cost per use) across subject disciplines and call number ranges can be used for assessment.
- ✓ Shared plans offer the just-in-time and not the just-in-case approach, which is becoming a fixture of collection development in many libraries.
- ✓ Shared plans are cost effective and therefore a desirable option for library administrators when determining collection budgets.
- ✓ All e-books generating costs to the library by default have been used.

and work together as a team. It is sometimes difficult for libraries to find consensus, and decision making or progress on a collaborative project can be slow. A collaborative UDA plan requires that the library group develop profiles, parameters, workflow, and other details with the vendor or vendors; thus, communications between the library group and vendors must be clear and efficient. Despite these challenges, many libraries are running successful UDA plans in a collaborative environment. Many UDA e-book plans are proving to be cost effective and beneficial to participating libraries.

Setting Goals

Goals of shared plans usually revolve around one or more of the following: enhancing collective collection building; utilizing shared or individual library budgets; developing efficient workflows that reduce staff time and overhead for individual libraries; acquiring a discount from publishers or vendors for participating as a group; and offering more content to users than is affordable by individual libraries using traditional acquisitions methods. Sometimes the goal can be simply to see how shared UDA might benefit a library group (Davis et al., 2012; Shepard and Langston, 2013).

Library Representatives and Working Groups

One key decision in the goal-setting phase is for the libraries to determine a representative or representatives from each participating institution. It is highly recommended that

PHASES OF IMPLEMENTATION

There are four phases for the implementation of shared and consortia plans.

1. Set goals and objectives:
    - Choose a representative(s) from each participating library and/or charge a committee or working group.
    - Decide on collection strategies and establish a budget plan.
    - Choose the type of UDA model to use.
2. Select a vendor or vendors:
    - Develop a formal or informal vendor evaluation and selection process; the process may include an official intent to negotiate (ITN) or request for proposal (RFP) procedure.
    - Negotiate with publishers.
    - Set terms and sign contract and license agreements.
3. Collaborate with vendors and aggregators:
    - Create profiles and parameters.
    - Review backlists and run test MARC record loads.
    - Determine technical workflows.
4. Launch and postlaunch:
    - Load discovery file; check links and platform functionality.
    - Monitor early uses for problems or issues.
    - Determine methods for reducing duplication.
    - Determine what parameters and technical workflow may need tweaking.

early in the planning stages someone from every library be the designated main representative or facilitator for the project. Representatives usually serve on working groups or task forces during the course of the project and must routinely send reports, information, questions, and issues back to their library stakeholders and staff. For some of the larger libraries, assigning a librarian—such as a collection manager or collections coordinator—to handle the collection development component might be advantageous. For large or ongoing projects, it is advisable to have a committee or working group established to implement, monitor, and manage the UDA project.

Collection Strategies

A major aspiration for a library group or consortia is to decide on the collection strategy. For EBA planning, the library group must decide on the publisher and content that will benefit all participants at an affordable cost. For DDA plans, the access versus ownership question must be discussed and agreed upon by all involved. Is the group's main goal to provide users with increased temporary access to content through short-term loans? Theoretically, a DDA plan could be set to provide access to a wealth of e-books for users and remove the purchase aspect altogether—that is, each e-book would be made available to users through short-term loans (STL) only. Is the group's motivation to purchase new titles for the permanent e-book collections that have demonstrated use? A plan can be designed to purchase an e-book on the very first access. If instead the goal is to blend access and ownership, a plan can offer both elements by allowing a few short-term loans before the last use triggers a purchase.

Budgeting

The available budget goes a long way in determining the boundaries of a shared UDA e-books plan. If there are long-term aspirations for a shared UDA plan, developing a budget strategy and method of allocation is recommended. Many shared plans are designed with a central deposit account from which the vendor deducts the cost of usage and purchases. More recently, vendors are extending a "pay as you go" billing option that allows libraries to pay for plans on monthly or quarterly installments instead of making large deposits. There are also other budgeting options for consortia, for example, paying for short-term loans from a central fund while each library pays for the triggered purchases individually based on usage.

Whatever billing options are decided, a library group or consortia has to devise a method to share the cost of UDA. A simple method is to divide the allocation equally among the libraries participating in the shared plan or pilot. Dividing the costs equally is fine for libraries in a group that are similar in size, but often libraries participating in a consortium vary in size and budget, so it behooves the group to develop an allocation system that is fair for each member.

Shared plans will not save libraries money per se, but a shared UDA plan can provide a method of stretching dollars and using funds more judiciously. Although shared DDA plans can be tweaked and the spend rate adjusted moving forward, the model can be problematic for budgeting since usage fluctuates. This is one reason the EBA model is growing in popularity, as it is far more consistent for library budgeting. Deposited funds are used to purchase e-books on an agreed-upon time frame (e.g., quarterly), so expenditures do not fluctuate. Negotiations are fairly straightforward: the more funds a group is willing to put into a deposit for purchasing e-books, the more content a publisher is going to make available. When a consortium has a more modest budget and no certainty of ongoing funding, it might be advisable to launch a pilot or short-term plan. Budgeting for a use-driven acquisition pilot or short-term (e.g., one year) shared plan is relatively simple, as often the participating libraries all contribute an equal portion of funding.

Models of DDA

The National Information Standards Organization (NISO) has identified three major use-driven DDA models for acquiring e-book content: the multiplier model, the limited-use model, and the buying club model (NISO, 2014). All three models employ the basic design for DDA programs where MARC e-book records are loaded into each participating library catalog, or a union catalog, and usage generates short-term loans and/or purchases of the e-books based on a use trigger. The multiplier model allows shared access and costs, but a multiplier is essentially where a library group or consortium pays the agreed-upon "multiple" times the list price for each e-book purchased after a predetermined number of uses. Short-term loans (STLs) are often included in the multiplier plan with the costs usually shared across the group. The limited-use model was developed by the Novanet consortium in Canada, allowing purchases at list price but with restrictions on usage, and has exhibited success (Duggan and Slauenwhite, 2014). The buying club model is based on a traditional consortium collection tactic where group purchases receive discounts, but each institution purchases and accesses e-books separately.

Hybrid models are also offered by aggregators and book vendors; these are plans that include various elements of PDA/DDA and even EBA models (and often include both print and e-book formats) merged together to meet a library group's specific needs. An example of a hybrid is a multitier perpetual purchasing model developed by the OhioLINK consortium that includes an e-approval plan, an e-book DDA, and other e-book collection purchases with three large publishers (Hoke and Silverman, 2014). Hybrids are becoming more common, but the DDA multiplier model is often included in the resulting mix of acquisitions methods. Clearly, the goals of a shared plan must take into account the model. For example, a consortium using the buying club model should receive purchasing discounts and not shared access.

Selecting a Vendor or Publisher

After goals are developed, the next step is to select the vendor. Selecting a vendor is an important decision, so libraries should do their homework. Librarians can review articles in library literature, monitor listservs and library blogs, and query colleagues on their consortium's experiences working with various vendors and UDA programs. Librarians can also look at e-book aggregators and book vendors' brochures, handouts, and websites to get an idea of the products and services they offer. Much of the initial information vendors distribute is generalized and intended for marketing and to provide libraries with a rough idea of a UDA program. For more details on how a UDA plan can be created to meet the requirements of a library group or consortium, librarians should develop questionnaires based on the goals for the plan and interview the vendors.

Hurdles of Vendor Selection

Frequently libraries or consortia are required by state or university contract rules to execute an official request for proposal (RFP) or intent to negotiate (ITN) vendor solicitation. The RFP or ITN process inevitably slows the selection of a vendor and can delay the implementation of a shared plan by several months. Even without the constraints of a formal ITN or RFP, the process of vendor selection usually requires each invited vendor to submit documentation and examples of UDA plans they offer. Often libraries will use checklists and establish criteria for the vendor selection phase. It is highly recommended that librarians request vendors to do an onsite presentation that details the UDA products and services they specifically can offer the consortium.

The number of vendors and aggregators in the library market that can offer the level of service, infrastructure, and publisher contacts to manage a large shared plan are few indeed. This limited field of vendors is not ideal, but at least most of the libraries collaborating on a shared UDA project will have had experience using one or more of the vendors. This experience and knowledge of the library marketplace is invaluable and can help determine the right choice of vendor. However, when a library consortium meets for the final time to discuss and vote on the vendor(s) to employ for the UDA plan, it will be difficult or even improbable to reach consensus. In this case, all participating libraries should be agreeable with the final selection and work with one another and the vendor(s) to make the project successful.

WHAT TO EXPECT FROM VENDORS

E-book aggregators offer

- DDA programs with hundreds or thousands of e-books across a range of subject disciplines from a multitude of publishers
- The ability to create parameters and profiles, including those for subject-specific content
- A platform for e-book navigation and access
- A system where purchases and short-term loans can be adapted to meet a group's goals for access and ownership
- Experience creating shared plans and workflows
- Invoicing, usage reports, and other technical capabilities

Book vendors offer

- Experience partnering with libraries in collection development
- More robust profiling, for example, targeting content by readership level
- Knowledge of creating and managing approval plans that is applicable to UDAs
- Methods to manage acquisitions streams (firm ordering, approval plans, and other UDAs), and to de-duplicate content
- A central database that coordinates communications, workflow, invoicing, and reporting across a library group

Negotiating with Publishers and Setting Terms

A critical step in creating a shared plan is determining which publishers are willing to participate in a UDA, shared e-books plan that offers content both appropriate and affordable for the group's collection and budgetary goals. Negotiating and contracting with publishers to participate is a complex and somewhat problematic stage in the creation of a shared UDA plan. Unless the library group is developing an evidence-based acquisition or selection plan directly with the publishers, negotiations are usually handled by the e-book aggregator or book vendor. There are growing complications with publishers over shared DDA e-book plans that are using the multiplier model. A number of publishers are either unwilling to participate or offer all their e-book content to a shared use-driven acquisitions plan (Emery and Parks, 2012).

There are several factors in a DDA shared plan that must be negotiated, such as the multiplier. Often book vendors or publishers gather statistics on the number of copies of the publishers' titles sold in previous years to a consortium to help define the multiplier and/or purchase trigger. Some publishers worry the DDA shared model will not generate sufficient profits so are hesitant to offer their premium e-book content to a shared plan. Although many publishers will participate in shared DDAs, their partial or full participation varies based on parameters of the plan. Other factors taken into account by a publisher are the size of the library group or consortium and the total number of users that will be accessing the e-book content.

The ultimate terms of the agreement have a substantial impact on the parameters of the use-driven plan. Publishers willing to participate in a consortia e-book DDA often insist on a multiplier large enough to generate revenue from sales they feel would be lost in a shared plan. Because of these complicated negotiations, setting firm deadlines for the negotiating process can be unrealistic. The design of a shared DDA is determined by which publishers are agreeable to shared plans and the terms they set for their participation.

The old cliché "what comes first, the chicken or the egg?" can describe the strategy of designing a shared plan, establishing parameters, and signing on publishers, as publisher participation is vital to the design itself. Consistent buy-in and support from academic publishers is essential for shared plans to be successful long term.

Once the publishers and vendor or vendors are selected, and the basic structure and terms of the plan are negotiated and agreed upon by all parties, a contract (and licenses if needed) can be drawn up, issued, and signed by participating members of the library group or consortium. Sometimes there are delays in this stage as often libraries must route large contract and license agreements through university legal or accounting offices for clearance.

Collaborating with Vendors

Many libraries within a consortium vary in size, budget, and mission. Forging a shared e-books plan for such a diverse group of institutions where all agree on parameters and budget allocations can be a daunting task. With multiple libraries involved, it is best to keep any shared plan simple. It is beneficial in early discussions if the library group can arrive at common ground on the overlying larger components of the plan, such as determining the scope and readership level of the e-books being accessed but at a cost that is affordable. In this complicated landscape it makes sense for libraries to partner with aggregators and vendors to develop practical and effective parameters and profiles of a shared plan. It is worth noting that many aggregators do not have a standard consortium "cookie-cutter" model; rather, they will provide a model and offer options that are best suited for that specific library group to meet its goals.

Setting Profiles

Defining parameters and creating profiles is the cornerstone to a UDA plan. Stages in determining profiles are similar to creating approval plan profiles:

- Choose the subject disciplines to be covered and user base (readership level) to be supported by the content received.
- Select the nonsubject parameters such as language, price caps, and imprint years.

For more details on setting parameters and profiling a DDA e-books plan, see chapter 4, "Demand-Driven Acquisitions (DDA)."

Devise Workflow

An attractive feature of shared e-book plans is the moderate technical maintenance required by the participating libraries, once UDA is in full operation. Getting to the operational level is the challenge. Staff at the individual libraries may be responsible for loading the initial and subsequent files of e-book MARC records sent from the vendor or publisher into the individual library catalog. New files may be supplied weekly, monthly, or quarterly by the vendor or publisher depending on the parameters of the plan. At scheduled times, staff will send updates of their library catalog holdings back to the vendor. The consortium may have centralized the processes of loading monthly or weekly MARC records into the union catalog and discovery services, as well as uploading the aggregate holdings of the consortium. Centralized record maintenance and loading is usually more efficient and demands less staff time for the libraries in a consortium. Nevertheless, the consortium should keep an eye on the workflow and duplication rate as the danger of centralization can result in lax monitoring of the plan by each participating library.

Reviewing and Modifying the Plan

Once the records are loaded and the shared plan is in operation, it is sure to require some troubleshooting and modification. Usually technical aspects are the cause for problems, but fortunately they are usually moderately small and fixable. For both EBA and DDA shared plans, the MARC records loaded into the catalog(s) should be checked immediately for functionality and problems. Users not being able to access e-books in the catalog or discovery tool via links to the aggregator platforms can create frustration and a headache for librarians across a consortium.

Libraries should check for duplication, and providing vendors with the catalog holdings for the libraries in the consortium should reduce duplication significantly. When duplicate titles are found in a library's catalog, the staff must have a mechanism in place with the vendor to remove them. If record loading and removal of discovery records are a centralized function, the consortium must communicate quickly to the appropriate staff to have the duplicate records removed. Library groups can expect that some adjustments will need to happen, but usually the problems encountered are not insurmountable.

After launching a shared UDA plan, a library group can expect that some modifications will be required. This is especially true of a shared e-books DDA plan; based on rates of cost and usage, the profiles and parameters may need massaging. One easy method to expand or limit content is with imprint years. Adding more years increases the number of e-books included in the plan; restricting years will lower the number of e-books offered to users. Another key component that has a bearing on the size of a DDA plan is the number of publishers included or excluded. Factors such as choosing a readership level or including and excluding subject areas are also methods to increase or reduce the e-book consideration pool. Even choosing or eliminating subject areas can have an effect: if a plan includes e-books that are classified in medicine or the science, technology, engineering, and mathematics (STEM) fields, the list prices are usually more expensive on average than e-books classified in the humanities. There is always the option for a library group with a large budget to keep profiles modest or tight with a goal of keeping the UDA plan in operation for a longer time.

Most technical modifications that will be needed can be minor, such as an individual library altering its own order workflow to reduce duplication. It is recommended that a library consortium have a task force or library representatives charged to monitor the plan after launch to ensure that content and expenditures are appropriate and meeting goals of the plan. To forge a successful ongoing shared plan, libraries should work as a team with vendors and publishers to make changes as needed. Chapter 11 of this book is devoted entirely to assessment and should be consulted for in-depth methods of analyzing use-driven plans.

Key Points

This chapter illustrates the phases and steps required to implement shared use-driven acquisition plans designed to acquire e-books. Here are the main points to remember:

- The components of a shared e-book DDA plan are basically the same as the DDA plan designed for an individual library, but shared plans are more complicated as there are multiple libraries involved that often range in size and collection needs.
- Libraries should consider collaborating with partners and incorporate use-driven acquisition programs into their collection strategies, but it is imperative that the objectives and budget plan are defined clearly for all participants.
- Shared plans require ongoing and clear communications between the consortium and the vendors and aggregators.
- Shared and consortia UDA plans are sometimes bound by rules—such as when an ITN or RFP must be fulfilled—that can be radically different from UDA plans created and managed by one library working with a publisher or aggregator.
- All parties—libraries, vendors, aggregators, and publishers—must benefit from the shared plan to warrant its launch and long-term sustainability.
- For DDA shared plans, negotiating a deal with publishers is necessary and sometimes tricky. The results from negotiations between libraries, vendors, and publishers have a great influence on the plan. Matters to negotiate include the number of uses that trigger a purchase, the multiplier on list cost, and in some DDA plans, the percentage of the list cost charged for each short-term loan by each publisher.
- Devising a cost-sharing methodology that is fair to all participants is sometimes difficult as often consortia and partner libraries differ in size, user base (FTE), and available material budgets.

The next chapter will describe the patron-driven acquisition (PDA) model for print materials.

References

Davis, Kate, Lei Jin, Colleen Neely, and Harriet Rykse. 2012. "Shared Patron-Driven Acquisition within a Consortium: The OCUL PDA Pilot." *Serials Review* 38, no. 3 (September): 183–87.

Duggan, Lou, and Bill Slauenwhite. 2014. "A Consortia PDA Program for E-books: Report of the Pilot Project." Presented at the OLA Super Conference, January 31. http://aleph2.novanet.ns.ca/.

Emery, Jill, and Bonnie Parks. 2012. "The Demand Driven Acquisitions Pilot Project by the Orbis Cascade Alliance: An Interview with Members of the Demand Driven Acquisitions Implementation Team." *Serials Review* 38, no. 2 (June): 132–36. doi:10.1016/j.serrev.2012.04.008.

Hoke, Sarah, and Deb Silverman. 2014. "Collaborative Collection Development." Presentation to the Florida Statewide University System (SUS) Collection Advisory Committee, November 17.

Levine-Clark, Michael. 2013. "Demand-Driven Acquisitions in the Colorado Alliance of Research Libraries." Presented at the American Library Association Annual Conference, June 30. http://www.slideshare.net/.

NISO (National Information Standards Organization). 2014. "Demand Driven Acquisition of Monographs: A Recommended Practice of the National Information Standards Organization." June 24. http://www.niso.org/.

Shepard, Jodi, and Marc Langston. 2013. "Shared Patron Driven Acquisition of E-books in the California State University Library Consortium." *Library Collections, Acquisitions, and Technical Services* 37, nos. 1–2: 34–41. doi:10.1080/14649055.2013.10766345.

Suggested Reading

Arch, Xan, Robin Champieux, Susan Hinken, Emily McElroy, and Joan Thompson. 2011. "By Popular Demand: Building a Consortia Demand-Driven Program." *Proceedings of the Charleston Library Conference*. http://docs.lib.purdue.edu/. doi:10.5703/1288284314974.

Emery, Jill, and Bonnie Parks. 2012. "The Demand Driven Acquisitions Pilot Project by the Orbis Cascade Alliance: An Interview with Members of the Demand Driven Acquisitions Implementation Team." *Serials Review* 38, no. 2 (June): 132–36. doi:10.1016/j.serrev.2012.04.008.

Richardson, Jeanne. 2013. "The Arizona Universities Library Consortium Patron-Driven E-book Model." *Insights* 26, no. 1 (March): 66–69. doi:10.1629/2048-7754.26.1.66.

Scott, Kerry, Jim Dooley, and Martha Hruska. 2013. "Collective Collection Building and DDA." *Proceedings of the Charleston Library Conference*, 457–61. http://docs.lib.purdue.edu/. doi:10.5703/1288284315306.

Library Case Study: Florida State University Libraries

Reporting: Roy Ziegler, associate dean for collection development

Type of institution: Public; space grant, sea grant

Memberships: Association of Research Libraries (ARL); Center for Research Libraries (CRL)

Faculty: 2,000

Students: 41,477, includes 9,000 graduates

Consortium: State University System of Florida (SUS)—consists of twelve public universities in Florida; Association of Southeastern Research Libraries (ASERL)

Colleges/programs/research centers supported: sixteen colleges, several research centers

Libraries: Strozier (main), Divac Science, Pepper Center, Allen Music, Goldstein, Law

Materials budget: fiscal year (FY) 2014–2015: $7.6 million (excludes medical, law, music, and satellite campuses), FY 2013–2014: $8.9 million (includes all university libraries)

Number and type of UDA plans: four plans; two plans at Florida State University (FSU) only, two shared: Wiley's local plan is managing an evidence-based acquisition e-books plan, with hundreds of e-books loaded into the catalog, $100,000 worth of books to be purchased over two years, and $50,000 deposited each year. Yankee Book Peddler (YBP) has just implemented an e-preferred approval plan. The shared SUS state PDA is participation in a shared PDA with the largest library consortium in Florida; partnering with Ingram-Coutts, the plan has been in operation over a year and cost-usage results are positive. One big hurdle for the plan is dwindling publisher participation—many are not on board or offering limited content to a shared plan.

The shared Cambridge usage-based plan is $30,000 (est.) deposit account to purchase permanent access to e-books after one year. Jointly profiled with the University of Florida (UF), but purchases are separate.

UDA budgeting: $150,000 allocated for all plans

Reasons for incorporating UDA: The decision to participate in PDA/DDA was made at the library administration level. There was concern the library had too many print and electronic books in the collection with little or no use, so there was support for usage-based models. When the FSU library introduced the possibility of PDA for print collections, it was received with an entirely new set of concerns. FSU has tabled the print PDA idea until the vendor can provide better workflow and assurances that books included in the plan will not go out of print.

Stated goals: Essentially the goals of our library and consortium's PDA/DDAs have been similar:

- Offer the maximum amount of content at reasonable prices.
- Provide generous access and usability.
- Show other institutions it is possible to collaborate for a common interest.
- Create efficient workflow and processing for library staff.

UDA and collection and budget strategies: UDA is incorporated into FSU's collection development strategy but is not yet incorporated into current written policy documents. The library's participation in shared projects is providing increased content to FSU users for the funds spent. The library reallocated approval plan funds for UDA.

UDA workflow and maintenance: Much of the technical requirements are centralized by the state organization overseeing the consortium's integrated library system, and budgeting is simplified by deposit accounts with vendors, so engaging in UDA saves the FSU library significant staff time.

Issues: The FSU-UF patron-driven acquisitions shared plan experienced a set of problems when several large publishers abruptly pulled out of the plan due to a contract dispute, and both libraries lost access to thousands of e-books. Thousands of discovery records had to be removed immediately from the libraries' catalogs, causing a flurry of complaints from users and reference librarians across the libraries. From the technical services side, there were major issues, but the biggest loss was from the collection development side from loss of content.

Challenges of UDA, Both Local and Consortium Plans

- Subject area librarians had concerns and continue to ask questions, but they are generally in support of the program because the materials are not charged against their accounts and they are more comfortable now that the plans are working.
- Because e-books don't currently represent all that's being published, there's a huge gap in the collective collection. Institutions within the consortium need to establish print-collecting responsibilities for specific subject areas.
- The idea of having a single collection for the consortium can be a hard sell at the institutional level. It's easier for electronic materials but can be very controversial when dealing with print collections. Getting a consortium to agree to a collection development policy for books (both print and electronic) will be challenging.

- Communicating a changing collection development strategy from a library to a consortium back to university administrators, faculty, and students is an important consideration that is often overlooked. Librarians need to share the reasons for the strategic change.

Success of the UDA Program(s)

Pros: FSU is looking forward to working directly with publishers that do not charge short-term loans (STLs) that have few DRM restrictions.

Cons: FSU believes the PDA/DDA model is not a stable collection development plan, so there are tradeoffs on having demonstrated use prior to purchase: multiple STLs drive purchase costs upward of 200 percent over the list price of a print book; and the STL model between publisher, aggregator, and library is very much in flux, and this volatility and uncertainty can be disconcerting.

Recommendations for Other Libraries

- Have an exit strategy for when a PDA/DDA plan ends for pulling out individual titles or the entire collection not yet purchased.
- Have a plan for accessing quality reports, and designate individual(s) to gather and distribute the information.
- For libraries embarking on shared plans, be mindful of the institutional politics and be willing to compromise and find the middle ground to keep the project alive. All parties need to know that the plan will benefit their institution.
- Shared or consortia PDA plans are just one tool among many to achieve the benefits of shared and/or consortia collective collections. There are plenty of economic incentives to support usage-based decision making for multi-institutional groups, but there are revolutionary and radical changes that come with the shift from just in case to just in time. The benefits can be a huge asset to the institutions involved, but different layers of complexity are inherent with any new model.
- Usage-driven acquisition is an important method that will help libraries be more sustainable, acquire a greater amount of content, and be more relevant to students and faculty.

Part 3

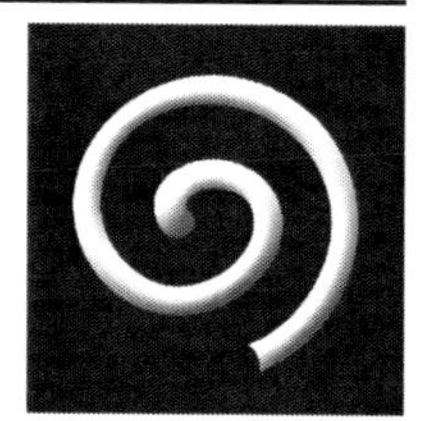

TARGETING LIBRARIES AND COLLECTIONS

CHAPTER 7

Patron-Driven Acquisition of Print Materials

Trey Shelton

IN THIS CHAPTER

- ▷ Providing a background for print PDA
- ▷ Implementing a print PDA plan
- ▷ Creating workflows for print PDA
- ▷ Evaluating the print PDA plan

THIS CHAPTER WILL FOCUS ON THE PLANNING and implementation of print-format patron-driven acquisition (PDA) plans. It provides background information on print PDA plans in academic libraries and discusses issues surrounding the development of these plans, such as content selection, technical setup, and evaluation. This chapter also includes two case studies as examples of how a large public academic library and a small private academic library are implementing print PDA plans.

Background on Print PDA

Print PDA plans are similar to e-book demand-driven acquisition (DDA) and evidence-based acquisition (EBA) plans in that records are loaded into the catalog and purchased based on patron input, or in this case a request to order. Instead of actual use, purchases are predicated on patron's self-reported, intended use, typically via a submitted request to the library. Print PDA plans differ from the purchase-on-demand (PoD) plans discussed in chapter 8, "Interlibrary Loan—Purchase on Demand (PoD)," in several ways.

FEATURES OF PRINT PDA PLANS

- ✓ Print PDA plans proactively anticipate needs, while PoD plans react to expressed needs of the user, such as demand-driven acquisition.
- ✓ Print PDA plans offer only print-format materials, while PoD plans have the potential to offer purchases for any format.
- ✓ Print PDA plans allow materials to be discoverable next to other library holdings, while PoD plans rely on the patron to discover the material elsewhere and inform the library of its existence.

One plan cannot meet the needs of all patrons. A complementary, holistic approach that incorporates multiple use-driven acquisition (UDA) plans with various formats and subject areas should be considered. Print PDA plans are best suited for situations where electronic materials do not meet users' needs, where electronic formats are unaffordable or unavailable, or when perpetual ownership and archiving of a print copy is a concern. Some libraries may want to offer e-book UDA content in a print PDA to allow users a choice in format, though many libraries may not have the budget to support such duplication and will focus on each plan that offers unique content.

Implementing a Print PDA Plan

As with all UDA models, there are many factors to consider when developing a print PDA plan. To begin, print PDA plans most commonly provide access to print monographs, though materials in any tangible format could be considered, providing discovery records can be obtained or generated. Most libraries use vendors with profiling and MARC delivery abilities. Librarians are familiar with the content selection and purchasing parameters of print PDA plans, but they may be unfamiliar with the notion of having unowned print items display along with readily available print books in the catalog. Be sure to communicate any changes in the catalog to librarians and public service staff as they will be fielding questions from patrons. Lastly, print PDA plans offer a cost-effective method of increasing users' access to print-format materials that a library may otherwise not be able to outright purchase and can complement or replace existing traditional print collection development plans (approval/slip plans and individual selection).

Goals

It is very important to consider the reasons the library is interested in developing a PDA plan specifically for print materials and how such a plan may fit into the larger mission, vision, strategic directions, and/or goals of the library itself and the parent institution. Print PDA plans may also play a role in consortia collection development plans, utilizing central funding models or cooperative collection development agreements.

From a practical standpoint, a library may wish to develop collection goals that focus on a specific discipline or subject area, particularly if it has been identified as an area of strategic importance or where print materials are required or preferred. This is often the case with subjects or disciplines that rely on image-heavy content. Alternatively, a library may wish to develop a print PDA plan that covers all subject areas. Plans covering a broad range of subjects are often incorporated into other UDA or traditional collection development plans. In addition, print PDAs have the potential to completely replace traditional collection development plans, such as approvals and/or slip plans, depending on the goals of the library.

Content Selection

Profiling for a print PDA plan is very similar to profiling discussed in chapter 4, "Demand-Driven Acquisitions (DDA)." It is common for a library to convert or alter existing approval and slip plans for use in print PDA plans. For libraries with no existing plans to alter or convert, creating a new profile is a fairly painless project. While large academic book vendors are capable of providing coverage for most English-language monographs, depending on the subject area and content type, it may be necessary to work with foreign or specialty vendors.

Not all book vendors actively support, or are fully aware of, print PDA plans. Although it is technically possible to develop a print PDA plan without vendor support, it is highly advisable to partner with the vendor to build and implement the plan. A vendor has the capability to provide assistance with profiling, technical setup, and workflow review that can be invaluable to the success of a plan. However, if a vendor is unwilling to actively support such a plan, librarians should consider what alternatives or workarounds might be possible to launch the plan without vendor support.

Budget

When planning the budget, print PDAs usually require less funding than a traditional approval or slip plan. The exact budget will be dependent on the amount of content in the plan. It is possible to fund a PDA by converting an approval and/or slip plan to a print PDA plan. Vendors with experience supporting print PDAs may be able to offer estimates as to the amount of funding needed to cover a particular print PDA profile.

QUESTIONS FOR VENDORS

- Do you support print PDA plans?
- What level of support is offered for MARC records services?
- Is there a minimum deposit?
- Can out-of-stock content easily be excluded?
- What is the average delivery time for orders?
- Do rush orders incur extra costs?
- What fulfillment reports are available?

Devising Workflows

Implementing a print PDA may be much more complex than other UDA models. Librarians need to consider how patrons will discover and request materials, how the library will respond to and process those requests, and what internal and vendor workflows can be redesigned to fit the plan's needs. The burden of technical infrastructure and setup to handle requests is shifted to the library, whereas UDA plans for electronic resources rely on vendors or content providers for most technical infrastructure, such as content platform/website, usage, purchase/short-term loan (STL) triggers, and loans/downloads. Print PDA plans require special handling and separate rush ordering.

Request System Design

At the fundamental level, a print PDA requires that records for the content should be discoverable in a library's catalog and/or discovery system. Those records provide some method for the patrons to request orders, where the request is sent to and acted upon by either library staff or the vendor directly, and then to notify patrons of availability. Print PDA titles need to clearly indicate that the title is not owned but can be requested. Figure 7.1 shows how a library catalog displays to users neither holdings nor call number information, only a message "Request this book" with an embedded hyperlink.

There are several methods for providing patrons with the ability to request items once they have discovered a record in the print PDA plan. The most obvious methods may involve using existing request features in the library's catalog or discovery system. However, such features may need to be altered to meet the needs of the print PDA plan. For example, requests for print PDA materials may need to be routed to different staff members for processing than would normal requests for owned items. Another method would be to build a custom request system or website, which would allow the library to potentially exert more control over the features and processes of the request system. Systems typically use title-level customized URLs in each discovery record that link users to the request system from the point of discovery, transporting essential bibliographic information to the request-form display in the process.

Some vendors are willing to assist in creating and adding the URLs to the MARC records they deliver. Libraries will need to work with vendors to establish the URL standards. Application program interfaces (APIs) can utilize metadata in the URL to display and pass on additional information. For example, the vendor ProQuest Coutts offers an API that uses ISBNs to look up the stock status of items in their warehouses. Libraries can use this information to inform patrons of how long it might take for an item to be received or pass the information along to acquisitions staff if stock status would alter internal workflows. Other APIs may also be incorporated that provide book jacket and Google Books link display. Print PDAs should allow access to the same set of users that any e-book UDA plans would, and authenticating users should be an important consideration. Figure 7.2 is an example of how the University of Florida Smathers Libraries designed a form for requesting a book purchase that includes a sign-on requiring user authentication.

Workflow Design

The patron should receive a confirmation, typically via e-mail, after his or her purchase request has been received by the library. The ordering processes for print PDAs should

1. Musikalischer Sinn
Boris Yoffe.
Author: Yoffe, Boris
Published: Hofheim : Wolke, 2012.
book

Request this book.
UF See Link to Request
add print email txt export

2. Alltagsklange - Einsatze einer Kulturanthropologie des Horens
Jochen Bonz.
Author: Bonz, Jochen
Published: Wiesbaden : Springer VS, 2015.
book

Request this book.
UF See Link to Request
add print email txt export

3. Von Richard Wagner zu Adolf Hitler Varianten einer rassistischen Ideologie
von Hubert Kiesewetter.
Author: Kiesewetter, Hubert
Published: Berlin : Duncker & Humblot, 2015.
book

Request this book.
UF See Link to Request
add print email txt export

Figure 7.1. Print PDA item display in catalog. Created by Trey Shelton.

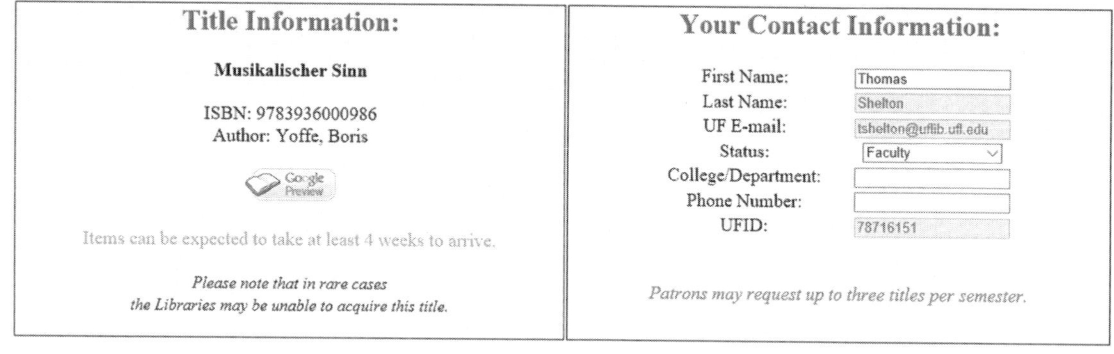

Request This Book

The University of Florida does not own this title. However, you may request that the George A. Smathers Libraries purchase a copy of this title to be added to the collection by completing and submitting the form below.

Title Information:

Musikalischer Sinn

ISBN: 9783936000986
Author: Yoffe, Boris

Google Preview

Items can be expected to take at least 4 weeks to arrive.

Please note that in rare cases the Libraries may be unable to acquire this title.

Your Contact Information:

First Name:	Thomas
Last Name:	Shelton
UF E-mail:	tshelton@uflib.ufl.edu
Status:	Faculty
College/Department:	
Phone Number:	
UFID:	78716151

Patrons may request up to three titles per semester.

You will be notified via your **official UF e-mail address** once the item arrives and is available for pick-up.

Submit Request

Figure 7.2. Print PDA item request form. Created by Trey Shelton.

follow the same processes the library uses for rush firm orders with a notification request. Order data can be delivered back to the library in the form of order-level brief MARC records, similar to many firm order workflows. Though the initial profiling should remove the need for content mediation, libraries may want to mediate print PDA orders in other ways, such as setting limits on the number of requests per patron per semester or year, or they may not want to implement API ordering.

Each library should discuss ordering, processing, and shipping workflows with their vendor in detail. Cataloging and shelf-ready services can often delay the shipment of materials to the library. A library should weigh the benefits of having the materials processed shelf-ready or having the materials shipped quickly unprocessed. In most cases, a library will probably rush catalog and process materials with a quick turnaround time. Once the material is available for checkout, the patron should be notified of its availability. Coordination with circulation and access services staff is essential to ensure that workflows and technical processes are seamless and painless for the patron.

Discovery Records

Most libraries will work with vendors capable of delivering MARC records based on the print PDA profile. The quality of the metadata in the MARC records will greatly influence the discoverability of the materials. Libraries should weigh the benefits and costs of having vendors enhance discovery records. Loading print PDA discovery records is very similar to loading MARC records for other UDA plans and should follow whatever standards the library has set for such records sets. As always, it is important to be able to effectively manage the records set, adding, updating, and deleting titles as necessary. Should the plan cease, the staff should have a plan to quickly pull all records from the system.

Evaluation

Any evaluation should begin with reviewing the goals of the plan to determine the metrics on which success should be based. A low volume of purchases or a slow rate of purchase are not necessarily indicators of a failed plan, especially if the goal of the PDA was to increase access to materials or to purchase only those identified as highly likely to be used. However, if usage of the plan is too low, it may not be a useful method of collection building for that particular situation. Print PDA analysis mimics the PoD plan analysis in many ways. Delivery turnaround times, number of requests, subject areas supported, and cost per item are all important metrics to evaluate.

The cost per circulation of print PDA purchased materials tends to be considerably lower than print monographs purchased via traditional means, especially when you take into account the oft-cited research that a significant amount of print monographs purchased by academic libraries are never checked out. Because use of print materials may not be as frequent as electronic materials, librarians should review this metric only after sufficient time has passed for circulations to accumulate to levels worth reviewing. Librarians may wish to review lists of titles profiled and requested through the PDA to ensure the content meets the standards the library has set. Profile changes can be made in consultation with vendor representatives to narrow or expand generated discovery content.

User surveys offer an alternative method of evaluating the plan. Questions geared towards the users' experience and satisfaction may provide the most insight. Some examples of questions might include the following:

- Was it clear that the library did not own the item you were requesting and would need to order it for you?
- Was it clear that this was a free service the library offered?
- Did you receive the item within a reasonable amount of time?
- Did the item you requested meet your needs?
- Would you request another item using this service?

Key Points

A print PDA plan is an excellent method to augment existing collection development efforts for print materials and anticipate patrons' needs for materials unavailable or inappropriate for an electronic format. Here are some key points to remember:

- Print PDA plans are commonly used for monographs but could be adapted for almost any format.
- Print PDA plans can complement e-book UDA plans and can complement or replace traditional print collection development plans.
- Vendors can help with many technical and content-selection aspects of print PDA plans.
- Much of the technical setup and maintenance burden rests with the library.
- Ordering processes mimic existing firm order processes, but additional automation options may be available.
- Evaluation of print PDA plans is similar to PoD plans.

The next chapter will focus on purchase-on-demand programs in an interlibrary loan setting.

Library Case Study: University of Arizona Library

Reporting: Stephen Bosch, materials budget, procurement, and licensing librarian
Faculty: 2,591
Students: 40,791
Type of institution: Public land grant
Memberships: Association of Research Libraries (ARL) and Association of American Universities (AAU)
Consortium: Greater Western Library Alliance (GWLA), Association of University Language Centers (AULC), Amigos Library Services
Colleges/programs/research centers supported: twenty
Materials budget: $11,593,400
Number of UDA plans: six
Reasons for incorporating print PDA: To ensure that materials purchased are those of highest interest to users. To improve the return on funds spent to purchase, process, and house print materials.
Key parameters of the print PDA profile: The print PDA materials includes nearly all types of print books including hard and paperbound, with a preference for hardbound books. The profile used was the former approval plan profile including all items that

would have been supplied as books on the plan as well as all titles that would have been treated as selection forms (slips).

Implementation: The print PDA was implemented using project management methodology. The first step was to create a communications plan to alert our campus to the changes, focusing on three key user groups: students, faculty, and administration. The library made sure that information about the project was readily available to staff involved, including a means of providing updates. Establishing and testing ordering workflows and creating a system for patrons to request items were major components of our implementation. Establishing and reviewing the PDA profile and resulting MARC files were also important aspects. The library also reviewed all the reports made available by either the vendor or the local system, which helped the library assess what types of material were being requested, the cost and circulation of each title, and the plan as a whole, including fulfillment rates and turnaround times.

Policies and strategic directions: The library has changed all of the collection management plans to incorporate the use of UDA plans.

Budget: The library currently allocates $200,000 annually on print PDA, which is funded using former approval plan funding. This funding represents just under 2 percent of the library's total materials budget. To date, the number of requests has never exceeded the budget. As the selection pool grows larger, the library expects that the total allocated amount will be expended and added funds may be needed in the future.

Technical hurdles: The library experienced many technical challenges during this project. Because the library did not want to mediate the plan in any way, allowing patron requests to trigger purchases automatically with the vendor, technical infrastructure had to be built by both the library and the vendor. Technical processes around the purchase process (receiving new bibliography, order, and items at the point of purchase as well as the setting of holdings in OCLC) also had to be discussed.

Patron experience: All items available for selection are in the catalog and in the discovery layer (Summon). Once the user finds a selection record, he or she will notice that instead of a call number and location, the book has a note that states, "Available for Order." There is also an 856 link that states, "Have the library purchase this book for the collections." Once the link is clicked, the user must authenticate using a university ID, as only authorized users may buy books. Once the link is activated, the supplier will receive the order request and will do a stock check, alerting the user to how long delivery will take. Once the book arrives at the library, it is placed on the hold shelf for patron pickup.

Evaluation: In the beginning, there was considerable pushback from our subject librarians; however, now that we have data showing how the program has succeeded, there is growing acceptance of the program. The library monitors what is purchased and compares this to the selection pool. Overall use of the materials and information on users is also gathered. This helps with analysis around which user groups use the service the most. Reports on the content pool and purchased materials are available from the vendor, but the library also uses data that is generated in-house to evaluate the plan.

Maintenance: Very little maintenance has been required so far beyond regular file loads and holdings updates. There have been instances where a system has changed or a better workflow was determined, which, of course, have ripple effects in the related processes. Overall, print UDA plans are generally lower maintenance than managing traditional firm ordering and approval workflows.

Successes: Overall, the program has been very successful. Since 2011, 115,125 (50,000 print, 65,125 e-books) titles have been added to the catalog for selection purposes, and over the past three years 15,220 titles were purchased (6,744 print) at a cost of $1,363,408. By comparison, the last year that the library had an approval plan, $1,116,803 was spent for 13,723 approval books. The former approval plan supplied about 275 new books per week; the DDA program now adds over 700 new selection records per week. As of early spring 2014, the 6,744 print books purchased in the plan had 11,802 checkouts with 5,996 renewals. The former approval plan averaged about a 52 percent circulation rate after four years. In contrast to previous purchasing plans, three times the content is available to users, at one-third the cost. The circulation rate for the print materials is four times that of the former purchasing plans.

Library Case Study: Drake University Library

Reporting: Teri Koch, head of collection development, and Andrew Welch, integrated systems project librarian

Faculty: 291

Students: 4,460 full-time enrollment (FTE)

Type of institution: Private

Consortium: Iowa Private Academic Libraries (IPAL); Central Iowa Collaborative Collections Initiative (CI-CCI)

Colleges/programs/research centers supported: College of Arts and Sciences, College of Business and Public Administration, College of Pharmacy and Health Sciences, School of Education, School of Journalism and Mass Communication

Number of UDA Plans: two

Reasons for incorporating print UDA: The library had previously implemented electronic UDA several years ago (with EBL), which we found to be useful and successful. It was important to include print materials in the UDA model given that there are still a large number of monographs that do not get published in electronic format, or if they do, the pricing makes it prohibitive to purchase.

Key parameters of the print UDA profile: The profile generated a total of 15,358 records. The profile integrated print and e-book content. If an e-book is available for DDA, the record is sent; if not, a record for the print title is sent after a ninety-day waiting period. If the e-book costs 130 percent more than the print formation, the print record is sent. Stock status is also taken into consideration.

Implementation: A soft launch of the program was piloted with only content applicable to the four professional programs (business and public administration, journalism and mass communication, education, and pharmacy and health sciences). After several months of piloting the program, content for the College of Arts and Sciences was loaded.

Budget: The library currently allocates $9,000 annually to the plan. This represents approximately 0.05 percent of the print monograph budget. This funding was reallocated from a traditional monograph budget line.

Technical challenges: Integrating the vendor's APIs with the library's request system was challenging because we were the first library to implement the APIs in that specific manner. There have also been issues with the print UDA profile generating content for titles already ordered via a different stream. The likely cause is the schedule for uploading holdings to the vendor's system. Initially the profiles were too restrictive, which resulted in too few titles in the catalog for users to discover. The profiles have since been expanded to include a wider range of titles. There have also been some issues with record delivery and item availability.

Patron experience: The patron discovers the book in the catalog or discovery service (like any other book). Instead of indicating a shelf location, the catalog note says, "This book is available On Demand," which is linked to a "Request this book" form. On the form itself, there is an embedded API that will perform a real-time stock check to determine the title's availability. If the title is in stock, the patron will have the option to request "rush" ordering. If the title is not in stock, the patron will not have that option.

Evaluation: The library has not yet evaluated the plan based on circulation or usage of purchased materials. Administrators are supportive of a UDA program that makes more effective use of budget allocations. There has not been any pushback from librarians and/or faculty about building collections with UDA. Firm orders for materials that are needed are still accepted.

Maintenance: Very little maintenance is required. From the perspective of an acquisitions associate, print UDA plans are much easier to manage than traditional order streams.

Successes: The plan has been moderately successful.

CHAPTER 8

Interlibrary Loan—Purchase on Demand (PoD)

IN THIS CHAPTER

- ▷ Justifying a purchase-on-demand program
- ▷ Establishing workflow for purchase on demand
- ▷ Preparing the groundwork for launch of a purchase-on-demand program
- ▷ Developing a purchase-on-demand program
- ▷ Ongoing evaluation of a purchase-on-demand program
- ▷ Identifying consortia purchase-on-demand programs

THIS CHAPTER WILL USE the phrase *purchase on demand* (PoD) for acquiring books through the library's interlibrary loan department (ILL). PoD purchases derive exclusively from patron requests, distinguishing them from other use-driven acquisition (UDA) models such as evidence-based acquisitions (EBA) or demand-driven acquisitions (DDA), where books or collections are loaded into the library catalog for patrons to discover. Conversely, ILL-PoD is a patron-driven purchase model whereby patrons request books not owned by their local library, and based on various criteria as discussed in this chapter, the book is purchased for the patron rather than borrowed from another library. The chapter will begin with a brief description of the traditional interlibrary loan processes and provide different options of how to establish a PoD that would be successful for your type of library environment. A successful PoD plan takes into account criteria for purchases, budget, workflow, working with other library departments, and how to best promote the program to your library patrons. This chapter also provides helpful tips for project management of people and workflow and how to create reports. Three library case studies are included to exemplify the unique implementation of PoD programs.

Why Launch a PoD Program?

There are many positive aspects to running a purchase-on-demand program using ILL requests as the basis for acquisitions. The foremost reason is that it is a successful method for collection building. Several articles in the library literature describe how PoD programs have been used successfully for augmenting standard acquisition streams, notably firm order purchases and books acquired on approval. An entire special issue of *Collection Management* focused on patron-driven acquisitions with several articles devoted to aspects of PoD. Kristine Anderson and colleagues (2010) published a study conducted at Purdue University on print books acquired by their PoD program in the liberal arts and concluded that it was an advantageous tool for developing collections. A follow-up study conducted at Purdue focused on science and technology books acquired through PoD, stating that the program was a successful way to augment collection building (Bracke, 2010).

In addition to filling gaps and building collections, books received through the Purdue PoD program showed higher circulation rates as compared to books purchased through traditional selection channels (Nixon and Saunders, 2010). Another study at the University of Nebraska, Lincoln, also revealed that books acquired by their PoD program circulated at higher rates (Tyler et al., 2010). Yet another reason to launch a PoD program is the cost-effective use of library funds. Studies have been done showing that the cost of interlibrary loan borrowing is not insignificant (Jackson, 2003; Leon and Kress, 2012). Thus, libraries might consider an alternative use of the book budget. Instead of using staff time and funds to borrow books not held in collections, libraries could use appropriate patron requests as a tool for collection building.

REASONS TO IMPLEMENT A POD PROGRAM

- ✓ Patron-initiated book purchases can fill collection gaps and target trending titles.
- ✓ Patron-initiated books added to library collections are a great supplement to traditional acquisitions methods such as approval plans.
- ✓ Many PoD programs can acquire a book in the time it takes to borrow through ILL.
- ✓ Many purchased books will circulate again.
- ✓ PoD programs are a relatively cost-effective use of library funds.
- ✓ PoD programs can purchase books despite budget freezes sometimes placed on traditional purchasing streams.
- ✓ Highly detailed reports and statistics can be gathered, including patron status, department, title purchased, type of book purchased, and cost of purchase.

Establishing PoD Workflow

One of the most attractive features of a PoD program is the flexibility. PoD programs can be implemented and managed exclusively in the ILL department, or in collaboration with the acquisitions department. Each option requires a different set of workflow, policies, and procedures. The main decision prior to implementation is which department will do the purchasing: ILL or acquisitions. The choice of this decision is library specific as it depends on several factors including staffing, library culture, and the overall organization of services and departments. If made through the ILL department, purchases can be easily submitted through the ILL workflow by sending the request through the vendor's OCLC symbol. If the purchasing is completed through the acquisitions department, a special queue in the ILL system can be created and the purchase request can be routed to acquisitions via e-mail. Another option is to train an acquisitions staff member to use the ILL system (e.g., ILLiad), but it would promote more collaboration if every effort is made to make this new workflow process easy on everyone. Often libraries will follow another library's preestablished workflow for implementing PoD; however, the flexibility of the model allows a library to adapt and develop a unique ordering workflow. Ultimately, the best and most appropriate workflow is dependent on an individual library's department organization, staffing available to manage the program, and ordering systems that are in place.

Before Launching a PoD

When a library decides to implement a PoD program, it is advisable to start on a small scale, often with a pilot program. The PoD program will modify workflow and staff assignments for the entire department or library, so a slow introduction may be received more positively by staff. The first step is to conduct your own research on a variety of interlibrary loan PoD programs in both the ILL and collections/technical services literature. Attend or participate in conference sessions, or join a professional organization for ILL, such as the Reference and User Services Association's Sharing and Transforming Access to Resources Section (RUSA STARS) of the American Library Association (ALA), to network with colleagues. With these great resources, you can contact libraries that are running PoD programs to see if they are willing to share their documentation on policies, workflow procedures, and assessment strategies.

Another valuable resource is to engage in conversation with colleagues in different departments at your library. It is important to obtain support from other departments, since they will ultimately be involved and their workflow will also be modified. It is best to start with administrative support, followed by department heads, librarians, and staff. Once you have made known your intentions to establish a PoD, form a task force in your library to drum up support for your initiative. Be sure to include people who may feel threatened with or are opposed to a PoD. If they feel that their concerns are being heard, you can work together to incorporate some of their ideas, or perhaps scale back certain aspects until you can demonstrate patron satisfaction, purchases in their collection areas, and so forth. Be sure to include library faculty or staff in cataloging and acquisitions to determine workflow and to create new workflow patterns. Once a task force has identified parameters for a PoD initiative, it's time to create a small-scale pilot project that outlines the goals and objectives, criteria for purchase selection, and workflow changes. Do not forget to inform everyone, especially reference and circulation staff, when the program will commence as these are the colleagues who will receive questions about the program. Therefore, it's advisable to hold information sessions for your library colleagues.

Developing a PoD Program

The best way to ascertain if PoD is right for your library is to initiate a pilot program. A pilot gives the library the time to monitor a PoD for workflow, cost, and turnaround time. A PoD program must take into consideration many factors, including the budget and staffing. If the funding support is robust, the program can be designed as an ongoing program with wider parameters for ordering. The larger your library, the more people will be involved and the longer it may take to establish a program. The smaller the library, the fewer number of people are involved, but this may have the greatest impact on changes in workflow. When establishing a new PoD program, it can be very helpful to use project management tools as outlined in chapter 1, "Use-Driven Acquisition Project Management." Phases and steps in implementing a PoD program are shown in table 8.1.

Phase 1: Set Goals and Objectives

It is important to identify goals for a PoD program. First, you will need to get support from librarians whose primary responsibilities are to build the collection. Share your pilot project goals and objectives with them and ask them to participate in a task force to establish criteria for purchases. When meeting with librarian colleagues, come prepared and demonstrate the need for a PoD program. It can help to share basic ILL borrowing statistics such as patron status, department, and title of book requested. It is equally important to stress that the PoD program will serve as a supplement to and not a replacement for collection building.

Table 8.1. Checklist for implementing a PoD program

PHASE	STEPS	CHECK AS YOU GO
Phase 1: Set goals & objectives	1. Identify desired metrics (e.g., users, titles purchased) 2. Identify budget options 3. Get "buy-in" from the library	□ □ □
Phase 2: Define parameters	1. Meet with subject librarians 2. Select format (e.g., print, e-book, language) 3. Determine users who can place requests (e.g., faculty, grad students, staff)	□ □ □
Phase 3: Devise workflow	1. Develop ordering system (e.g., Amazon) 2. Create a budget plan 3. Designate staff responsibilities 4. Determine type of delivery method to users 5. Create reports (e.g., summative and formative assessment)	□ □ □ □ □
Phase 4: Launch & assess	1. Review titles purchased 2. Keep track of budget 3. Analyze ordering and delivery time of materials 4. Conduct user survey	□ □ □ □

GETTING SUPPORT FROM YOUR LIBRARY

- Share your vision on why a program is needed.
- Identify the steps of implementation.
- Describe the funding reallocation.
- Demonstrate how it promotes cross-collaboration among departments and streamlines workflow.
- Show enthusiasm on how patrons have a unique opportunity to participate in collection building that directly supports their teaching, research, and education.

A good example of how to sell the program occurred in 2006 when the University of Florida Smathers Libraries initiated a PoD pilot program. The ILL librarian stated the following in the PoD proposal to library administration:

> This pilot project was touted as a patron-centric approach to supplement the current collection development program. The proposal also supports the 2006–2007 goals of the George A. Smathers Libraries to: "*build and manage library collections in support of academic programs; and provide timely access to requested material*" (Libraries Mission Statement). . . . This pilot program will also foster a collaborative cross-departmental relationship to better serve the research and academic needs of the UF community. (Foss, 2008)

It is important to set attainable goals. A couple of reasonable goals for a small-scale pilot are to verify if the program is affordable and kept within budget, and if purchases support the scope of collections. Another goal is to ensure that workflow is manageable and easy to follow. If your staff is spending too much time on ordering and processing, you will need to reassess the workflow. It is also a great idea to seek staff input on how they can contribute to the workflow revisions.

Phase 2: Define Parameters

After meeting with ILL staff and librarians and securing buy-in, it is time to create an advisory group to assist with the development of criteria for purchases. Examples of criteria to consider for purchases are as follows:

- Patron status. You will need to determine which patron requests should be considered for purchases, such as those of faculty, researchers, graduate students, distance patrons, and undergraduates. This is the time to be inclusive or exclusive.
- Lost or missing from the current library collection. If requested books are marked as "lost" in the library catalog, will they be purchased regardless of the patron status? This could be a great way to add materials back into the collection if they are requested frequently via ILL, and if the library does not currently have a lost replacement policy.
- Cost of the book. The cost of a book varies greatly depending on the discipline. Work with the librarians in charge of collections to determine the average costs of books. Books in the STEM (science, technology, engineering, and mathematics)

disciplines are going to be more expensive than books in other disciplines. Be sure to create a price range where all disciplines can participate in the program. For example, if you set a purchase price limit of $70, most STEM books will not be included.

- Type of material. Many times patrons will request textbooks and other materials required for class. Now is the time to decide if textbooks will be included. Other material types include theses, dissertations, conference proceedings, technical reports, musical scores, DVDs, foreign titles, out-of-print books, and "core" monographs.
- Readership levels. What type of books will this PoD include—popular fiction, nonfiction, textbooks, reference, lower undergraduate, upper undergraduate, graduate, or research?

When establishing parameters for PoD purchasing, verify that the purchased materials fit within the collection strategies of the library. If there is a decision to create a consortia PoD program, the same considerations for implementation can be used.

Phase 3: Devise Workflow

In this phase, the ILL staff and the staff responsible for cataloging and acquisitions will need to address workflow and operational issues. Discussions should include the need to create a temporary record in the catalog. When a book is ordered through the PoD program, the ILL staff should create temporary records in the catalog to avoid any duplicate purchases. Creating a macro of the necessary fields by the cataloging staff allows for a standardized protocol of MARC record data entry.

Many PoDs differ on how, who, and when to contact the patron once the material arrives. One option is for the patron to check out the book after it is rush cataloged (within forty-eight hours) with the library circulation date based on patron status (e.g., faculty, staff, and student). Another option is to check out the book to the patron immediately as a traditional ILL loan of two to three weeks, and once it's returned have it cataloged and placed in the collection.

The financial and budget analysis of a PoD program depends on how it is managed. If the PoD program is managed through ILL and only uses IFM (ILL fee management), the purchases are automatically charged through the ILL system. A monthly report can be generated through the system.

If the PoD program is operated jointly with the acquisitions department, it is important to establish how to keep track of costs and other relevant statistics. The ILL department is one of those departments that can be housed in either technical services or public services. Creating policies and procedures are dependent on current library operations. While some workflow adjustments will be made, the program will be more successful when there is as little disruption as possible to existing working operations.

If the PoD program uses a credit card, purchase card (P-Card), or invoices, purchases should be reconciled by the library finance department. A credit card or P-Card can be used for on-the-fly purchases or materials bought through online booksellers (e.g., Amazon). Invoicing is a process where the library makes a purchase and the vendor remits a bill.

Phase 4: Launch and Assess

To evaluate any program, formative and summative assessments are mandatory. Luckily, ILL systems provide a robust opportunity for data collection. For a PoD program, it is important to identify the type of information required to justify the continuation of the program. Statistics that are gathered from the ILL system (e.g., ILLiad or OCLC) can be easily shared and made relevant to all. Most importantly, the statistics must demonstrate that the program meets the goals and objectives. Examples of statistics to evaluate may include the following:

- ILL record number assigned to each request as it identifies the exact request and clarifies any confusion or duplication of titles requested
- Title of the book, which can determine how many times the title has been requested
- Patron status that identifies a person by patron type (e.g., faculty, student, or staff), department, distance education/online–only program, various regional campuses, library branch, and so forth
- Requested date of item (this can help determine the duration of the purchase process)
- Date shipped, which verifies the turnaround time from requested date to time of shipping
- Date received, which indicates when the material arrives at the library
- Cost of the book, including total fees for the month, which can easily be reconciled by the billing department

Tracking statistics in Excel will allow you to determine the breakdown of the purchases and fees per month during the pilot. You can also demonstrate if, for example, there is a steady increase in the number of orders per month. Keeping track of the cost will ensure that the pilot program will not go over budget.

Ongoing Evaluation

The PoD program must be evaluated on a continual basis. Internal assessment focuses on statistics and workflow of the program, while external assessment looks at patron satisfaction. Internally, the PoD program should gather purchasing statistics on a monthly basis with reports sent to the librarians/selectors. Depending on the length of the pilot or an established program, a formative assessment should be conducted midway through the cycle or semester. Costs, turnaround time, and patron-ordering patterns will reveal if and where modifications to the program are required. At the end of the pilot program or fiscal year, a summative assessment report should include costs, titles, patron status, patron department, and turnaround time for purchases. This report should be disseminated to all library staff.

Externally, if a decision is made to market a PoD program, expectations must be clearly defined. Be prepared, as some patrons will take advantage of the program to create their own research library. One solution is to insert a custom-made bookmark into the book asking the patron a few simple questions about their ILL experience and stating that the book has been entered into the library collection based on their request. This soft promotion informs patrons of their contribution to building a library collection and that the library is in turn supporting their educational and research initiatives. Sample bookmark questions include the following:

- Did the book arrive quickly?
- How useful is this book as a permanent addition to the library's collection?
- Do you want to check out this book once it's been cataloged? (Note: Only use if the patron is given immediate access to the book before cataloging.)
- Would you recommend this book to a colleague?

Gathering anecdotal evidence is a great indicator of whether the program is supported by the patrons. This quick survey should be part of the summative assessment. At the end of a pilot program or fiscal year, the ILL department and relevant library staff should host a meeting to determine if any changes should be made to the existing program.

Consortia PoD

Purchase on demand (PoD) is one of the earliest use-driven models and is still going strong in many libraries. Almost always the PoD model was developed for one library using patron requests from the interlibrary loan (ILL) department. Purchase on demand as a collection tool for collaboration is not widespread, but there are programs in existence worth noting. One pilot conducted in 2010 by the Consortium of Academic and Research Libraries in Illinois (CARLI) and the University of Illinois at Urbana-Champaign (UIUC) found success by offering a PoD across the consortium that purchased print books from user requests. More than sixteen thousand print book records were loaded into the union catalog, and staff at UIUC would rush purchase and ship books not available in the consortium. At the end of the pilot, 190 print books had been purchased and delivered to users in an average of three business days per request (Wiley and Clarage, 2012). Based on this early success, CARLI and UIUC partnered to launch a more ambitiously funded, print PDA pilot. Begun in 2012, over two thousand print book bibliographic records were loaded initially into the union catalog. CARLI funded the PoD, and UIUC managed the book ordering and delivery responsibilities for the project (CARLI, 2012).

With the overarching goal of combining demand-driven acquisitions with cooperative collection development, two librarians from the University at Buffalo (UB) cite three case studies their library conducted with partner institutions using the purchase-on-demand model of acquiring print books. The first case study describes a partnership with Empire State College where ILL staff from both institutions worked in conjunction. Books that met established criteria were purchased from ILL requests and delivered directly to users. The second case study described how, in 2010, libraries in the State University of New York (SUNY) consortium participated in a joint project where ILL-requested print books, meeting defined criteria and not held by any of the libraries, were purchased instead of requested on loan. All ten libraries contributed to a central fund, and by the end of the pilot, more than 750 books were purchased. The third case study was conducted in 2009 through UB's regional consortium, the Western New York Resources Council (WNYRC), with seven libraries participating in the project. Using established criteria that regulated selection, ILL requests that were not owned by any library were purchased rather than borrowed from outside the group. At the end of the first year of the pilot, more than 470 print books had been purchased. In all three of these case studies, the purchase-on-demand shared plans were deemed successful and a useful method for "expanding aggregate collections while reducing ILL costs" (Booth and O'Brien, 2011, 155).

Key Points

A PoD program can offer a positive and collaborative experience for all library staff. If the program is promoted, patrons and faculty can feel part of the collection-building process and may take a more active role in reviewing the catalog and recommending materials to add. Here are points to take away:

- Parameters can be established for ILL borrowing requests to acquire materials that fit collection strategies.
- A library should establish a separate and permanent budget for the PoD program, as collection managers will more readily support a PoD program if their materials budgets are left intact.
- A PoD program can be promoted to faculty and administration as a means to support the educational and research initiatives of the institution.

PoD programs are evolving as many are adding e-books and other material types, such as streaming videos. The next chapter will focus on how to incorporate a streaming-video program into a library's UDA plan.

References

Anderson, Kristine J., Robert S. Freeman, Jean-Pierre V. M. Herubel, Lawrence J. Mykytiuk, Judith M. Nixon, and Suzanne M. Ward. 2010. "Liberal Arts Books on Demand: A Decade of Patron-Driven Collection Development, Part 1." *Collection Management* 35, nos. 3–4: 125–41. doi:10.1080/01462679.2010.486959.

Booth, Austin H., and Kathleen O'Brien. 2011. "Demand-Driven Cooperative Collection Development: Three Case Studies from the USA." *Interlending and Document Supply* 39, no. 3: 148–55.

Bracke, Marianne Stowell. 2010. "Science and Technology Books on Demand: A Decade of Patron-Driven Collection Development, Part 2." *Collection Management* 35, nos. 3–4: 142–50. doi:10.1080/01462679.2010.486742.

CARLI (Consortium of Academic and Research Libraries in Illinois). 2012. "Patron Driven Acquisitions Project: Print Materials." Accessed March 10. http://www.carli.illinois.edu/.

Foss, Michelle. 2008. "Books-on-Demand Pilot Program: An Innovative 'Patron-Centric' Approach to Enhance the Library Collection." *Journal of Access Services* 5, nos. 1–2: 305–15.

Jackson, Mary E. 2003. "Assessing ILL/DD Services Study: Initial Observations." *ARL Bimonthly Report* 230/231.

Leon, Lars, and Nancy Kress. 2012. "Looking at Resource Sharing Costs." *Interlending and Document Supply* 40, no. 2: 81–87.

Nixon, Judith M., and E. S. Saunders. 2010. "A Study of Circulation Statistics of Books on Demand: A Decade of Patron-Driven Collection Development, Part 3." *Collection Management* 35, nos. 3–4: 151–61. doi:10.1080/01462679.2010.486963.

Tyler, David C., Yang Xu, Joyce C. Melvin, Marylou Epp, and Anita M. Kreps. 2010. "Just How Right Are the Customers? An Analysis of the Relative Performance of Patron-Initiated Interlibrary Loan Monograph Purchases." *Collection Management* 35, nos. 3–4: 162–79. doi:10.1080/01462679.2010.487030.

Wiley, Lynn, and Elizabeth Clarage. 2012. "Building on Success: Evolving Local and Consortium Purchase-on-Demand Programs." *Interlending and Document Supply* 40, no. 2: 105–10. http://www.emeraldinsight.com/.

Further Reading

Alder, Nancy Lichten. 2007. "Direct Purchase as a Function of Interlibrary Loan." *Journal of Interlibrary Loan, Document Delivery and Electronic Reserve* 18, no. 1: 9–15. http://dx.doi.org/10.1300/J474v18n01_03.

Carrico, Steven, and Michelle Leonard. 2011. "Patron-Driven Acquisitions and Collection Building Initiatives at UF." *Florida Libraries* 54, no. 1: 14–17.

Chan, Gayle Rosemary Y. C. 2004. "Purchase Instead of Borrow." *Journal of Interlibrary Loan, Document Delivery and Information Supply* 14, no. 4: 23–37. http://www.tandfonline.com/.

Herrera, Gail, and Judy Greenwood. 2011. "Patron-Initiated Purchasing: Evaluating Criteria and Workflows." *Journal of Interlibrary Loan, Document Delivery and Electronic Reserves* 21, nos. 1–2: 9–24. doi:10.1080/1072303X.2011.544602.

Hussong-Christian, Uta, and Kerri Goergen-Doll. 2010. "We're Listening: Using Patron Feedback to Assess and Enhance Purchase on Demand." *Journal of Interlibrary Loan, Document Delivery and Electronic Reserve* 20, no. 5: 319–35. doi:10.1080/1072303X.2010.517420.

McHone-Chase, Sarah. 2010. "Examining Change within Interlibrary Loan." *Journal of Interlibrary Loan, Document Delivery and Electronic Reserve* 20, no. 3: 201–6. doi:10.1080/1072303X.2010.492003.

Van Dyk, Gerrit. 2011. "Interlibrary Loan Purchase-on-Demand: A Misleading Literature." *Library Collections, Acquisitions, and Technical Services* 35, nos. 2–3: 83–89. http://dx.doi.org/10.1016/j.lcats.2011.04.001.

Ward, Suzanne M. 2012. *Guide to Implementing and Managing Patron-Driven Acquisitions.* Chicago: Association for Library Collections and Technical Services, American Library Association.

Ward, Suzanne M., Tanner Wray, and Karl E. Debus-López. 2003. "Collection Development Based on Patron Requests: Collaboration between Interlibrary Loan and Acquisitions." *Library Collections, Acquisitions, and Technical Services* 27, no. 2: 203–13. doi:10.1016/S1464-9055(03)00051-4.

Way, Doug. 2009. "The Assessment of Patron-Initiated Collection Development via Interlibrary Loan at a Comprehensive University." *Journal of Interlibrary Loan, Document Delivery and Electronic Reserve* 19, no. 4: 299–308. doi:10.1080/10723030903278374.

Zopfi-Jordan, David. 2008. "Purchasing or Borrowing." *Journal of Interlibrary Loan, Document Delivery and Electronic Reserve* 18, no. 3: 387–94. doi:10.1080/10723030802186447.

Library Case Study: University of Chicago Library

Reporting: Mary Radnor, document delivery services librarian

Program: The PoD at the University of Chicago is a very informal program. It is nonfunded and used as a last resort for purchasing books when borrowing options via interlibrary loan have been exhausted.

Budget: There is no official budget for this program.

Criteria: Any type of format or material that cannot be borrowed through ILL can be purchased through this program as long as the cost does not exceed $40.

Workflow: The purchases for books are through Alibris in OCLC. ILL requests are used as a last resort using IFM only. After the patron is finished reading the book, it is taken to the gifts area. Once in the gifts area, the collections librarians review the books in their assigned discipline and decide whether to add it to the collection. If the book is not added, the material is added to the library book sale. Although the patron is asked if the book should be added to the collection at the time of the ILL submission request, ultimately the collection librarian makes the decision for inclusion. Each week the collections librarians receive an e-mail notification to review books.

Assessment: It is estimated that two-thirds of the ILL requests are books and purchased through Alibris (fiscal year [FY] 2014: fifty-six purchases, mostly popular fiction).

Additional information: For articles, ILL does not use on-demand services such as Get It Now or ArticleFirst. Instead, requested articles are purchased directly from the publisher website, or from national libraries (e.g., British Library, etc.) using a credit card.

Library Case Study: The Ohio State University Libraries

Reporting: Brian Miller, head, interlibrary services

ILL and ILS system: ILLiad/Sierra III

Overview: Oversight of the PoD is managed on a day-to-day basis by the head of interlibrary loan. The fund manager of record is the collections strategist. Together, they establish the PoD guidelines.

Budget: The PoD budget in FY 2014 was $30,000. The actual amount spent was roughly $23,000 for 249 purchases, so not all of the funds were exhausted, but this is not unusual. The $30,000 PoD budget does not include health sciences purchases, but any request for a health sciences title is submitted to health sciences acquisitions, which has a parallel workflow.

Criteria: In this PoD, the standing rule of thumb is that the request will be purchased as an e-book, not hard copy, if available. The patron does not have a choice on format (i.e., print or e-book). Below are the criteria for purchases through the ILL PoD program:

- if videos or music scores are requested by faculty or if the student claims a scholarly purpose
- if the book is published or will be published within one week. If the title is not yet published, the patron is referred to the collection manager.
- if the book is published in the current year, or published in the previous year, until the start of fall semester
- if the book is not owned or on order by any Ohio State University (OSU) Columbus campus library location
- if the book is not available in OhioLINK, SearchOhio, CIC through UBorrow, or the Columbus Metropolitan Library (excluding regional campus patron requests)
- if the book is scholarly in nature
- if the book is less than $200

- textbooks if not already owned or on order. International editions may duplicate a regular edition but are essentially the same work (compare pagination and dates); prefer regular edition whenever possible, and should be placed on closed reserve.
- If the request is an exhibition catalog, ILL will attempt to borrow the material. If the material cannot be borrowed, the patron is referred to the fine arts librarian for purchase consideration.
- foreign language titles if immediately available as indicated on Amazon

Workflow: When the patron makes the request in ILLiad (ILL system), the routing rule takes any request published within the last two years to a custom queue called New Publications Review. Once in this queue, the request is reviewed by the head of ILL, who then decides on borrowing or buying. If the decision is to purchase, the request gets cancelled in ILLiad with e-mail notification to the patron that the title will be purchased instead of borrowed. The acquisitions unit (AU) is copied on the patron e-mail so they can initiate purchase. When the AU receives the e-mail, the request is processed as a rush through GOBI (collection management system). If the purchase is in print, upon receipt, the piece is immediately cataloged and labeled; then, a hold is placed in the patron's name and sent to the appropriate library pickup location (as denoted in original ILLiad request). If it's an e-book, the link to a newly created local catalog record is e-mailed directly to the patron.

Assessment: Every month, statistics are reviewed to make sure purchase-on-demand requests are filled. The statistics include how many were purchased by month, fiscal year to date, and compared to the same month and year to date of the prior fiscal year.

Final thoughts: A majority of ILL requests are in the humanities and social sciences disciplines. OSU does not receive many ILL requests for science monographs, perhaps due to the cost of the title. However, if an OSU patron requests a 2015 imprint of a science book for $300, the ILL department would attempt to borrow the material. If borrowing is unsuccessful, the patron is referred to the subject librarian for possible purchase using subject-specific funds.

Library Case Study: University of Nebraska, Lincoln Libraries

Reporting: Joyce Melvin, ILL borrowing and reserves manager

Enrollment: ~25K students

ILL and ILS: ILLiad/Sierra III

Budget: The PoD began as a pilot program (started over ten years ago) and continues pending approval on a yearly basis. In 2013, the budget was $50,000 per fiscal year, an increase over previous years. With the budget increase, the program could expand its purchasing parameters to include a variety of materials including DVDs, CDs, and electronic dissertations. The budget is part of the broad acquisitions budget. Since collection managers were satisfied with the type of content being purchased, this PoD program was given a recurring budget. The program is now considered one of three pillars of collection management: (1) ILL; (2) approvals; and (3) recommendations via liaisons.

Criteria: Under the PoD program, ILL staff may purchase fiction, poetry, DVDs, and CDs. Textbooks are excluded from purchase. The cost of the materials may not exceed $175.

Workflow: The PoD is mediated through the ILL office. The patron submits a request, and if the publication date is within the scope of purchase, it is routed to a purchase queue. A designated ILL staff member orders books through Amazon, CDs through ArkivMusic, and electronic dissertations through ProQuest. All ILL staff members are cross-trained for the PoD so there is never a delay with placing purchase orders. On the same day as the purchase, the ILL staff sends an e-mail notification of purchase to the acquisitions/cataloging staff. When purchasing e-books, this workflow is especially important because not all e-books are in the library catalog, so verification of title duplication is needed. After the material arrives in the library, it is rush cataloged and returned to the ILL staff, it is then updated in the ILLiad system within the document delivery queue, and the patron is immediately notified that the material is available for checkout. In the case of physical items, the material is circulated through the library ILS.

Assessment: As part of the review process, the delivery (ILL) services provide information on what was reviewed for purchase and if the item was bought. This report is submitted to the collection development committee during the course of the year. The ILL staff looks for patterns of requests and attempts to fill in the collection management/service holes.

CHAPTER 9

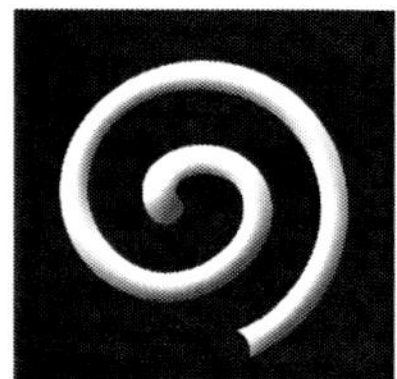

Streaming Video

Trey Shelton

IN THIS CHAPTER

- ▷ Providing background on streaming-video UDA plans
- ▷ Identifying models and content providers
- ▷ Implementing streaming-video UDA plans
- ▷ Marketing streaming video
- ▷ Evaluating streaming-video UDA plans

THIS CHAPTER WILL FOCUS ON THE planning and implementation of streaming-video use-driven acquisition (UDA) plans. It provides an overview of the landscape of streaming-video selection models and discusses factors to consider when developing a streaming-video UDA. Included is a case study example of how an academic library has approached these types of plans. In addition, spotlight interviews introduce readers to two vendors' perspectives on streaming-video UDA.

Background

Streaming video is a relatively new and increasingly popular format in academic libraries. By 2013, 70 percent of academic libraries offered streaming video, a 40 percent increase from 2010 (Farrelly and Hutchison, 2014). Such a shift may be attributed to increases in streaming-video requests from faculty for course reserves and online courses (Cross, Fischer, and Rothermel, 2014). Rachel King (2014) points out that while demand for streaming videos is on the increase, the title availability is limited compared to the diverse range of needs for popular and educational videos present in most academic settings. The

REASONS TO IMPLEMENT STREAMING-VIDEO UDA

- ✓ Supports distance-learning initiatives
- ✓ Provides unlimited simultaneous users
- ✓ Provides users with access to a large, diverse pool of video content
- ✓ Requires very little maintenance from the library once UDA is up and running
- ✓ Is a cost-intelligent model for acquiring access to video content; ensures return on investment
- ✓ Eliminates waiting for limited course-reserve copies
- ✓ Reduces DVD/VHS replacement/maintenance/storage costs
- ✓ Reduces need for DVD/VHS players
- ✓ Eliminates overdue fines or lost replacement charges
- ✓ Reduces time spent on acquiring and processing individual DVDs

licensing of single streaming-video titles has historically been a complex process and involves many departments within the library (Schroeder and Williamsen, 2011).

UDA plans to acquire streaming video are not currently prevalent in academic libraries, based on a 2014 survey that revealed that a mere 9 percent (n = 26) of respondents are running a patron-driven acquisition/demand-driven acquisition (PDA/DDA) plan for streaming video (UF Libraries, 2014, Q7). This is because streaming-video UDA is still relatively new to the library market, but librarians should expect the number of plans to increase sharply as assessment of early adopter library plans are more widely shared and discussed. Though UDA cannot completely solve the issue of limited streaming availability, it may simplify workflows and anticipate need, while also reducing the risk of purchasing unused content.

Models and Content Providers

The available streaming-video UDA models mimic e-book UDA models in name and function. Currently there are three vendors offering streaming-video UDA models: Alexander Street Press (ASP), Docuseek, and Kanopy Streaming Video. All three vendors focus on educational films and documentaries covering a wide variety of disciplines. Streaming-video models discussed in this chapter are patron-driven acquisition (PDA) and evidence-based acquisition (EBA).

It's important to understand your library's goals and to work with your vendors to understand what selection and licensing models are available to help meet those goals and fit your budget. The licensing and selection models described below are accurate as of the time of publication. Key features of each of the models described in this chapter can be found in table 9.1.

Evidence-Based Acquisition

The EBA models for streaming video are similar to EBA e-book models described in chapter 5, "Evidence-Based Acquisitions (EBA)." ASP and Docuseek are vendors that

Table 9.1. Streaming-video UDA models

VENDORS	UDA MODEL OFFERED	LICENSING OPTIONS FOR UDA PLANS	PDA PURCHASE TRIGGER	EBA MINIMUM COMMITMENT	TITLE SWAPS	PRICING MODEL
Alexander Street Press	PDA	one year three year perpetual (most titles)	Set number of playbacks	N/A	N/A	Varies by title
Alexander Street Press	EBA	perpetual	N/A	$34,000	N/A	Varies by title
Kanopy Streaming Video	PDA	one year three year	fourth use	N/A	N/A	Standard: one year, $150 three year, $350
Docuseek	EBA	one year three year (after initial one-year license)	N/A	200 titles (bulk pricing varies by institution)	Optional after two years	Tiered pricing with bulk discounts applied

offer an EBA model. EBA models require a minimum, upfront commitment but allow for access to large sets of content for a set period of time, no more than one year. The amount of content made available is usually proportional to the amount of the upfront deposit. The library then makes periodic selection decisions that are applied against the deposit. Usage statistics are provided to assist in the decision-making process, though selections may be made using any rationale or criteria deemed appropriate by the library. As Eileen Lawrence of ASP points out, "EBA is a nice blend of letting the patrons influence decisions, but letting librarians make the final selection" (see the second vendor spotlight).

Patron-Driven Acquisition

The PDA plans for streaming video closely resemble the demand-driven acquisition (DDA) e-book plans described in chapter 4, "Demand-Driven Acquisitions (DDA)." For libraries that are new to or considering adding streaming video, the PDA model offers the most flexibility, primarily due to no upfront commitment, and the flexibility to focus on a narrow or niche subject area. Vendors ASP and Kanopy offer PDA streaming-video plans that require no upfront commitment. These plans offer libraries the ability to customize their plan down to the title level, which ensures that only videos deemed appropriate for the collection are licensed. Purchases are triggered after a set number of uses of a title, generating a one- or three-year license to the film. Perpetual upgrade options may be available, depending on the provider and the film.

Implementation

Streaming-video plans require a similar level of effort to implement from a technical standpoint as e-book plans. In addition, once a plan is running, little maintenance is needed beyond maintaining MARC records and tracking purchases and usage. Plan evaluation may be somewhat more difficult than e-book plans, as librarians will likely have less historical cost-and-usage data to establish acceptable levels of return for their library than they might with e-book plans.

Goals and Objectives

With any collection-building decision, it is wise to align that decision with the goals and strategic directions of your library and institution. This will help to ensure that the content made available and eventually purchased will meet the needs of the users and may help build administrative support for the plan. Some libraries may focus a UDA plan around specific subject areas. This is also a good time to incorporate a DVD/VHS weeding project to save shelf space. Other goals to consider should be target dates and project planning, both of which should be discussed with the vendor and staff responsible for implementing the models.

Content Selection

The content that streaming-video vendors offer is quite diverse, though; just as with e-books, not everything is available and there is some overlap between providers. Libraries should be aware of which streaming content is already accessible to their patrons through subscribed or purchased collections before planning a UDA project to avoid duplication (if that is a concern). Libraries may also evaluate the catalogs of potential vendors to determine if multiple simultaneous plans are required to provide a holistic collection. Just as with e-book publishers, libraries should be aware that not all producers allow their content to be licensed for UDA plans.

Streaming-video plans are typically based on predefined collections from the vendor and do not involve a complex approval, plan-like profile. Subject and/or producer collections can be mixed and matched to fit the needs of your users and the goals of the plan, and vendors allow various levels of customization to the collections.

For some, even with the predefined subject categories, the content options may be overwhelming, especially if your budget is limited. There are practical approaches that can be taken to narrow the field of possibilities. Since many streaming-video requests seem to originate with faculty who need the film for a course showing or for course reserve, this may seem like a natural area to begin. Which courses request streaming content most frequently? Connecting directly with the faculty members who request the content or the subject librarian responsible for the faculty member's department may help in understanding the needs of users, ultimately making the plan more successful. In some cases, course reserve staff may know of certain courses, faculty members, or disciplines that request the most streaming content.

If few requests for streaming content have been received, users may be unaware of the library's ability to provide this format. Films on course reserve or with otherwise high circulation in DVD/VHS format may be reviewed to determine streaming availability and appropriate subject areas for inclusion in UDA plans. Yet another approach may be to focus on disciplines where film best meets the instructional needs of the classroom. For example, identify distance-learning initiatives on campus and tailor your program to those initiatives.

Before finalizing the plan, it is important to request or download a title list for each collection under consideration. This title list should be reviewed and approved by appropriate internal stakeholders, to ensure that content unsuited to the goals of the plan is not included. Vendors may also offer webinars to new customers to introduce them to the vendor's platform and selection and licensing options. Librarians can inform their vendor of their subject parameters either through a template form or via e-mail.

Budgeting

As with any new program, securing funding for streaming-video plans may prove to be challenging and require a certain amount of creativity. Some libraries, such as UNC Greensboro, may choose to divert funds allocated to physical film formats to a streaming-video PDA (see the library case study). Libraries accustomed to spending large sums on perpetual streaming-video collection purchases may find it easy to shift that spending to an EBA pilot. Librarians should also investigate the possibility of receiving funding from distance-learning initiatives and technology fee awards on their campus.

MARC Records and Discovery

The vendors discussed in this chapter all currently provide MARC records for loading into local catalogs and discovery systems. As with e-books, the quality of the records varies from provider to provider and title to title and is not always available for all titles. MARC files are usually downloaded from the vendor's website. If your library is new to the streaming-video format, you may run into unexpected issues. Just as with e-book plans, MARC records should be loaded to reflect any changes in accessible plan content, such as new, updated, and deleted records. Staff members responsible for loading records should have a plan to quickly identify and remove records loaded should the plan cease or drastically change. Streaming-video platforms should also be included in all discovery and access tools, along with other e-resources. Librarians should ensure that any database lists and discovery systems include streaming-video providers and content.

Once the details of the plan have been agreed upon, the plan must be implemented. License agreements should be reviewed and signed, and deposit invoices, if any, issued and paid. Deposit accounts offer many benefits, such as reducing the number of invoices to pay, but some libraries may prefer the limited commitment of the pay-as-you-go method. In addition, if the library has no previous relationship with the vendor, the platform, including librarian administrative access, must be configured.

Marketing

While e-book UDA plans are often not promoted, streaming-video plans may require a different approach. Some vendors strongly encourage their library customers to market their plans to the users directly, especially to faculty. Users may not be aware that the library offers streaming video for a variety of reasons. Librarians have observed the decrease in library catalog usage for quite some time. Even those patrons who do use the catalog may think that streaming videos would be more readily found in a database or website. To help combat the user's misperception, vendors may offer marketing packets geared toward the faculty in the subject areas selected for inclusion.

Faculty should also be made aware of the many features and tools of the streaming platforms that may assist them in teaching, especially in the online learning environment. For example, the ability to make clips and embed videos into learning management systems (LMS) is a popular feature. Librarians may wish to create a guide to streaming videos in the library, which may include examples of the features of each platform, the types of content included, and access details. Course reserve and other relevant library staff should be notified of the availability and asked to revise workflows or processes to take streaming-video content into account. The University of North Carolina at Greensboro used multiple marketing methods to engage faculty and students in their streaming content (see the library case study).

Evaluation

In many ways, evaluating streaming-video UDA plans is similar to evaluating e-book UDA plans. Librarians should consider the type of licenses purchased (one year, three year, and/or perpetual) and the UDA model (EBA or PDA) when assessing their plan, especially if multiple license types are being purchased or if swapping titles in and out of an EBA is involved. Vendors do offer multiple types of downloadable usage reports with cost information, but these data are discoverable in multiple reports and are not in a nice, clean single report for easy analysis. It is advisable for librarians to build or request reports and then analyze the plan as a whole, by subject or producer collections, or title by title. There are also COUNTER-compliant reports, which are common, and librarians may find non-COUNTER-compliant reports equally or more useful, depending on the level of granularity or aspect of the plan they are interested in. Usage statistics patterns can sometimes reveal high usage in unexpected subject areas that may lead to a change in the plan's content profile or identify highly used titles better suited for licensing outside of a plan.

Figure 9.1 offers an example of a streaming-video vendor report. The dashboard prominently features a combination line and bar graph detailing minutes viewed, number

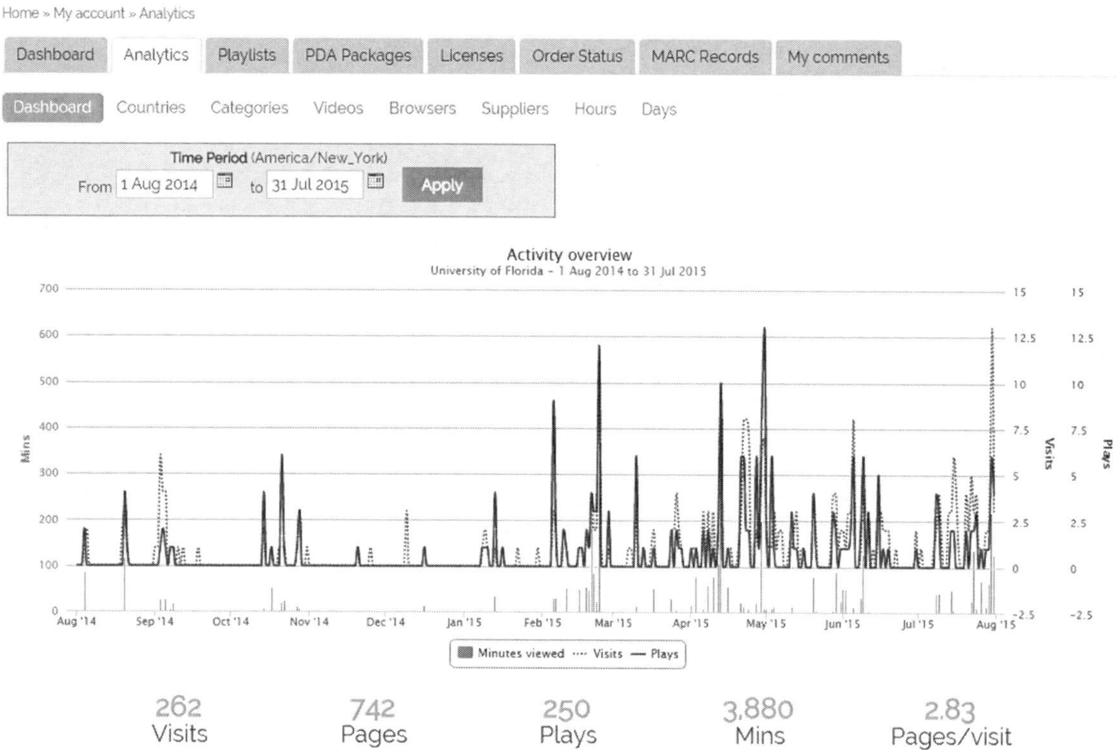

Figure 9.1. Example of a streaming-video usage report. Courtesy of Kanopy.

of plays, and number of page visits for any given date range. Below the graph there is a listing of each title that has been used on the platform during the set time frame, which can be exported into Excel. Libraries that have licensed collections or individual titles through non-PDA means will need to filter out those titles. A separate PDA dashboard also provides total page views, total video plays, total number of titles to be invoiced for the current quarter, and a listing of which PDA collections are activated.

To properly evaluate the plan, many factors must be considered. As with any e-resource evaluation, it may be challenging to determine what should be considered an acceptable return on investment (ROI) for your library. This is even more applicable for streaming-video UDA since the model is new, and little has been published on streaming-video UDA. To assist libraries in keeping track of plan metrics, vendors offer downloadable reports detailing accessible content, purchases, and license start and expiration dates; however, libraries may wish to also determine an in-house method for tracking the various elements of the plan. Perpetual purchases can be tracked with methods similar to those used to track other perpetual e-resource purchases, while one- and three-year licenses should be tracked using methods similar to those used to track subscription e-resources. These methods may include complex software such as integrated library systems (ILSs) and electronic resource management systems (ERMs) or simple spreadsheets.

Libraries should regularly track purchases of their UDA plans to ensure the rate of spending meets the library's expectations. Usage of both PDA and EBA plans should be monitored regularly during the phases of the plan. Cost-per-use reports are a standard measurement for determining if the plan is meeting goals. Streaming videos are no exception to the cost-per-use standard and will likely also follow the trend of increased focus on alternative metric analytics that other e-resource formats are experiencing. Videos purchased in perpetuity may take longer to reach the lower cost-per-use levels than one- and three-year licenses may produce. The use and potential cost of videos used but not purchased should also be incorporated into any analysis.

While vendor administrative platforms offer many useful features, the information is rarely synthesized into a report useful for holistic plan analysis. Table 9.2 is an example of a relatively simple cost-per-use report of purchased PDA titles in a relatively new plan. The report was constructed by merging information from two separate vendor reports. Such a report could be used to analyze title level and overall plan cost-effectiveness, becoming more informative as the plan progresses. Libraries may also wish to organize titles by subject collections when building similar reports. It is important to note that a holistic report that is more detailed often increases the number of vendor-provided reports you will need to merge.

Libraries may also wish to conduct qualitative analyses that focus on users' needs and perceptions. Formal or informal qualitative methods can be utilized to determine if the content meets the faculty's curricular needs, if students find the platform easy to use, if the content is easily discovered, where patrons search for streaming content, and other similar questions. Once the evaluation is complete, the internal stakeholders should holistically evaluate the plan to determine the plan's success and select titles if running an EBA plan. The library may wish to continue the plan as is, or make alterations of content or funding level.

Table 9.2. Example of a library-generated cost-per-use report

TITLE	LICENSE	COST	NUMBER OF PLAYS	COST PER PLAY	MINUTES VIEWED	COST PER MINUTE
Africa: Open for Business	1 year	$150.00	9	$16.67	19	$7.89
Consumerism & the Limits to Imagination	1 year	$150.00	12	$12.50	49.73	$3.02
Diversity and Multiple Identities with Ron Scott	1 year	$150.00	6	$25.00	19.08	$7.86
Family Matters: Family	1 year	$150.00	10	$15.00	107.92	$1.39
First Contact	1 year	$150.00	4	$37.50	23.43	$6.40
Forest of Bliss	1 year	$150.00	3	$50.00	1.89	$79.37
N!ai, The Story of a !Kung Woman	1 year	$150.00	4	$37.50	24.85	$6.04
Nanook of the North	1 year	$150.00	3	$50.00	14.88	$10.08
Numen: The Healing Power of Plants	1 year	$150.00	1	$150.00	4.98	$30.12
Nursing: Client Activities and Specimen Collection	1 year	$150.00	5	$30.00	8.54	$17.56
Race: The Power of an Illusion	1 year	$150.00	13	$11.54	203	$0.74
The Mask You Live In	1 year	$150.00	9	$16.67	307.85	$0.49
The New Modernists: 9 American Architects	1 year	$150.00	1	$150.00	1.09	$137.61
Tough Guise 2: Violence, Manhood & American Culture	1 year	$150.00	155	$0.97	4,165	$0.04
Plan totals		$2,100.00	235	$8.94	4951.48	$0.42

Key Points

Although streaming-video UDA plans are relatively new to academic libraries, they have quickly gained traction. Here are some key points to remember:

- Demand for streaming videos is increasing rapidly. UDA offers the ability to drastically increase access to streaming videos and ensures that only those films used are purchased.
- UDA plan goals should incorporate an institution's mission and strategic directions.
- Look to faculty requests and online learning initiatives for subject areas to focus on.
- Marketing the library's streaming videos is key to faculty adoption and can play a critical role in course reserve programs and meet various curricular needs.
- Streaming video reduces risk of loss or damage of DVDs, eliminates patrons' frustrations around having to check out DVDs, and delivers a format users are already comfortable with.

- Reallocate material budgets or seek funding from online education initiatives or technical fee awards to fund pilot programs.
- Evaluate plans regularly to ensure goals are being met and to determine cost-effectiveness and ROI.
- Libraries should use quantitative and qualitative analysis to determine if each plan is a good fit for the libraries' circumstances.

The next chapter will highlight the operation of UDA models in public and special libraries.

References

Cross, Cheryl, Christine Fischer, and Cathy Rothermel. 2014. "Streaming Film: How to Serve Our Users." *Serials Review* 40, no. 3: 154–57.

Farrelly, Deg, and Jane Hutchison. 2014. "Academic Library Streaming Video: Key Findings from the National Survey." *Against the Grain* 26, no. 5: 73–75.

King, Rachel. 2014. "House of Cards: The Academic Library Media Center in the Era of Streaming Video." *Serials Librarian* 67, no. 3: 289–306.

Schroeder, Rebecca, and Julie Williamsen. 2011. "Streaming Video: The Collaborative Convergence of Technical Services, Collection Development, and Information Technology in the Academic Library." *Collection Management* 36, no. 2: 89–106.

University of Florida George A. Smathers Libraries (UF Libraries). 2014. "UDA Library Survey." Last updated August 10, 2015. http://ufdcimages.uflib.ufl.edu/IR/00/00/71/94/00001/UDA_Library_Survey.pdf.

Further Reading

Alvin, Glenda. 2013. "How to Engage Faculty with Academic Video." *Against the Grain* 25, no. 3: 56.

DeCesare, Julie A. 2014. "The Expanding Role of Online Video in Teaching, Learning, and Research." *Library Technology Reports* 50, no. 2: 5–11.

———. 2014. "The Mass Market and Consumer Tools." *Library Technology Reports* 50, no. 2: 33–39.

Duncan, Cheryl J., and Erika Day Peterson. 2014. *Creating a Streaming Video Collection for Your Library*. Lanham, MD: Rowman & Littlefield.

Finlay, S. Craig, Michael Johnson, and Cody Behles. 2014. "Streaming Availability and Library Circulation: An Exploratory Study." *LIBRES: Library and Information Science Research Electronic Journal* 24, no. 1: 1–10.

Library Case Study: University of North Carolina at Greensboro Libraries

Reporting: Christine Fischer, head of acquisitions
Faculty: 1,005 full-time enrollment (FTE)
Students: 18,000 (undergraduate and graduate)
Type of institution: Public
Memberships: Association of Southeastern Research Libraries (ASERL), LYRASIS, Triad Academic Library Association (TALA), University Library Advisory Coun-

cil (ULAC), Council on Library and Information Resources (CLIR), Coalition for Networked Information (CNI), Coalition of Open Access Policy Institutions (COAPI), Center for Research Libraries (CRL), Evans Creation Partnership Text (Evans TCP), Folger Institute, Library Publishing Coalition, OCLC, Portico, and the Scholarly Publishing and Academic Resources Coalition (SPARC)

Consortia: Carolina Consortium and NC LIVE

Colleges/programs/research centers supported: seventy-nine undergraduate programs in more than one hundred areas of study, sixty-five masters programs, and thirty doctoral programs

Materials budget: $3,620,922

Number of streaming-video UDA plans: three (Kanopy Streaming Video PDA; Alexander Street Press PDA; Docuseek EBA)

Program overview: The University of North Carolina at Greensboro's (UNCG) shift to streaming video was the result of a convergence of factors. Requests for the format to the distance education librarian had been steadily increasing as many courses and degree programs were moving to the online environment due to both institutional mandates and budget issues. UNCG had and continues to use Swank Digital Campus for popular films, offered Films on Demand, and had purchased several collection sets from Alexander Street Press, but still had demand that wasn't being met. After purchasing one-year licenses to several films on the Kanopy platform, the library opted to start a PDA with Kanopy. UNCG is also running an EBA plan on the Docuseek platform, Docuseek2. The library has a history of purchasing DVDs from producers that Docuseek offered streaming licenses to, so it made sense to pilot the company's EBA. Finally, UNCG recently launched a PDA program with Alexander Street Press. The library found Alexander Street Press's PDA pricing comparable to other providers, and it offered a good alternative to buying large, perpetual packages.

Reasons for incorporating streaming UDA: In addition to the increased demand from faculty, students are accustomed to streaming video, and DVD in-building use has been considered passé for quite some time. The faculty also relies on streaming videos to support flipped classroom models. UDA has allowed experimentation with pilot programs that drastically increase access with a relatively small financial commitment. It can be difficult to secure streaming rights to some titles. The UDA programs help the library anticipate the needs of their users. Faculty members may discover the exact film they were interested in, a comparable film that suits the needs of their course, or a film they weren't expecting to find but is actually more appropriate for their course.

Budget model: UNCG has historically purchased films from both departmental firm-order budgets and a dedicated budget for films. UNCG has begun to reallocate some of the film budget to streaming video, including the UDA plans. UNCG finds streaming-video UDA plans fiscally sustainable because only content that is being used is licensed, there is little or no financial commitment, and plans can easily be shut down or paused at any time.

Content of UDA plan: Librarians were curious as to what sorts of titles might be used and decided the plans should offer a wide variety of content covering many subject areas. The titles that are heavily used tend to reflect those courses and programs already requesting streaming video. Women and gender studies, sustainability, and social justice are all disciplines that see high levels of usage. The librarians at UNCG are hopeful that the wide variety of content might help to intrigue faculty in other disciplines as awareness of the format's availability spreads.

Marketing: UNCG markets the content that the UDA plans make available to both students and faculty. The library has also reached out to the student health and sustainability units on campus to showcase to the library's streaming-video collections. These marketing efforts have done a great deal to bring a greater awareness to streaming video on the UNCG campus. As faculty have become more accustomed to streaming video, librarians have noticed an increase in faculty members' awareness of issues concerning public performance rights and fair use.

Access and discovery: UNCG utilizes the OCLC WorldShare Management Services as their ILS. MARC records are downloaded monthly from the Kanopy administrative dashboard. The MARC records are loaded into the system, and holdings are also tracked in the OCLC knowledgebase.

Assessment and reporting: UNCG's primary focus is to ensure that use levels are satisfactory and to determine ways to further boost usage. The library monitors usage reports provided by the vendors. Reports detailing top categories of use have spurred the library to license an entire producer's collection due to its high usage.

Challenges of UDA: The only challenges we have faced have revolved around access and discovery. The OCLC knowledgebase has also provided unique challenges, but none of the issues the library faced were overwhelming or significantly impeded implementing UDA plans. UNCG librarians would like to see a greater availability of streaming content through UDA plans, particularly with foreign feature films.

Successful thus far: UNCG's measure of success is based on use but does not rely on any arbitrary metrics. If faculty stopped finding the content valuable or if students stopped using the films, then the program would cease, but as long as activity continues to grow, these plans will be considered a success.

Vendor Spotlight: Kanopy Streaming Video

Interview with: Tom Humphrey, director of sales

What are some of the challenges of implementing streaming-video PDA plans from the vendor perspective? The biggest challenge has been education. With PDA, there are mechanics ("what triggers a film?") and administrative features ("how do we monitor this?") that need explanation and demonstration. Our PDA program also differs in important ways from e-book programs, and we have had to warn against making analogies or assumptions based on e-book experiences. This was particularly challenging in the earlier days when it was more novel; today, with so many case studies and libraries with long track records, it is a lot easier.

Do you require any minimum purchase commitments? No minimum requirements or commitments. Libraries set any budget, decide to deposit or "pay as you go," design their collection, and then only pay for films that are triggered. I think many libraries find the ability to take full control of all aspects refreshing.

Some libraries are concerned about spending their budget before year end, and a couple of things are important to understand. First, the program always involves multiple years of access, because even if you hit your budget and turn off PDA after ten months, access to triggered films (the most popular films) continues for the year(s) beyond. Second, we have built a seamless process for switching the program on or off—it can be converted to a mediated PDA or paused completely. Third, with so many libraries running programs, we have a good baseline of benchmarks to accurately predict spend. In essence, if we ever have a conversation about hitting your budget, this is both a good thing (you are guaranteed to have seen strong usage) and an easy situation to manage.

What about perpetual access? Ownership is an important consideration for any library, but I think many are now questioning at what cost. Beyond expense, perpetuity has two fundamental drawbacks. First, usage is unpredictable and value is temporal. Faculty and course requirements change, and the films used today are not necessarily the films demanded tomorrow. This is perhaps most pronounced in the health and sciences fields. We had to retire a film on CPR as the rules changed—it would have been potentially dangerous for a student to use the film as an educational resource. Second, there is growing demand for breadth. Faculty can be very particular about the films they need, and the volume of films available today is greater than ever before and growing. It is difficult for libraries to meet this demand and insist on maintaining perpetual rights on all streaming-video holdings. What we at Kanopy are seeing is a mindset shift from *just-in-case* to *just-in-time* collection building.

How do you assist your customers with plan evaluation? The best thing we can do is to connect libraries to discuss experiences. Ultimately, no matter how good we are at articulating the benefits of the program, there is nothing more powerful than hearing those same messages echoed from peer libraries. Once up and running, libraries look less to peers and more at their own experience for crafting and evaluating their plans. We provide an administrator dashboard with powerful tools for analyzing content, usage, and engagement. Inevitably this is complemented by qualitative feedback from users.

In what sorts of situations are streaming-video PDA plans most successful or unsuccessful? Kanopy works with libraries of all shapes and sizes, from colleges with ninety-eight students to the largest research institutions. The model is designed to work for every college regardless of the size or goals of the plans. PDA models democratize access to content—in the past, only richer institutions could afford many of these resources, and this is really shifting that paradigm.

How do you see streaming-video PDA evolving in the next five years? There is no question that streaming is growing faster than any other resource. More films are becoming available, students are responding strongly to it, and the faculty, especially the younger faculty, is willing to embrace it. We are dealing with a population that heavily relies on online video, and the library market is catching up with that. These changes boost PDA's relevancy—demand is becoming more diversified, varied, and unpredictable, conditions under which PDA thrives and is most nimble.

Another major shift is in how libraries assess value. In the past, libraries primarily focused on "volume value" (i.e., cost per item); today, we talk about "ROI value" (i.e., cost per play); and the rhetoric of the future will be "engagement value" (i.e., cost per *engaged* play), which incorporates information on how users engage with resources to build a picture of true impact.

Why should video producers participate or continue to participate in PDA models? Participating in PDA affords a number of benefits. Marketing films à la carte (as with DVDs) maintains the value of films but is expensive and exhausting as a sales process. Bundling films into collections is convenient but leads to heavy discounting of films. With PDA, we are combining the product convenience of collections with the financial attractiveness of à la carte.

Vendor Spotlight: Alexander Street Press

Interview with: Eileen Lawrence, senior vice president

What are some of the challenges of implementing streaming-video UDA plans from the vendor perspective? Alexander Street Press (ASP) knew that we wanted to offer demand-driven models because library behaviors are changing. We wanted to balance out considerations for the needs of libraries and the interests of the video providers and find the sweet spot. Because many librarians are concerned with perpetual access, we waited to go to market with our PDA while we negotiated with our information providers (IPs), or the rights owner. We are considering 2015 a pilot year for our PDA model, and things may change as we learn more. We spent a lot of time tweaking our EBA model during its pilot year, making changes to the administrative platform, for example.

Do you require any minimum purchase commitments? The EBA model does require a minimum commitment, which is based on the length of the plan. The upfront commitment is required because we have to compensate our IPs for up to an entire year's usage of video as titles are used. The final value of a video owned at the end of the plan is, of course, equal to the advance payment amount. The PDA plan requires no upfront payment.

What about perpetual access? The EBA model exclusively offers perpetual rights. The PDA model offers perpetual rights upgrades for a growing majority of titles, currently at least 75 percent of them. We wanted to build perpetual access into the plan because we have so many customers that believe perpetual access is the philosophical best choice.

How do you assist your customers with plan evaluation? The ASP administrative module provides daily usage statistics reports. We offer COUNTER4 compliant, SUSHI enabled, and customized usage reports. An account manager performs three- and ten-month check-ins with the customer to make sure everything is progressing as expected. We also use these consultations to review the plan to make sure the library is getting the best return. For example, sometimes it makes better financial sense to license an entire collection based on EBA or PDA usage.

In what sorts of situations are streaming-video UDA plans most successful or unsuccessful? When our sales team is discussing EBA and PDA plans with customers, we spend a lot of time talking about what would be the best match. For example, Brigham Young University (BYU) was a pilot customer for EBA, but they chose not to continue the plan because they preferred our collections and ended up using remaining EBA dollars to buy collections. But many other libraries have continued the plans, seeing them as great successes, selecting titles individually with funds that they would have spent on streaming video anyway. Ultimately, a blended approach may work best; for example, a library may support a strong history program where the best value is to buy a collection outright. The library may also support a small dance program where only one or two courses are offered; here the EBA or PDA allows libraries to select individual titles.

How do you see streaming-video UDA evolving in the next five years? Right now, I hear the term *Wild West* from our customers; they are confused. There are lots of models, and they do not know which to choose. I think that the IPs are watching closely now, and they will start modifying their behavior too, realizing that it is good for their exposure and sales. Some IPs will realize that PDA is the wave of the future but won't be able to tolerate free uses, and will want to invoice on the first use, while others may just adjust prices.

I think that some librarians will want to take back control over building collections. Librarians will still look at the math, trying to determine return on investment (ROI), but they can't just look at usage because all titles purchased in EBA or PDA are used. Also, one playback in a classroom, regardless of how many people were watching in the classroom, only shows as one use. ROI may begin to include factors such as impact on career planning, grades, and course ratings. We will be watching all of this. We may also need to start looking at short-term loans. It may be that short-term access is better for some videos instead of a one-year subscription. Also, we are working to make our profiling more sophisticated.

For ASP, EBA may become more popular than PDA. PDA is fascinating and new, but EBA may win out, especially for those customers interested in perpetual access. EBA is a nice blend of letting the patrons influence decisions but letting librarians make the final decisions. Also, EBA will always be able to offer more titles—currently EBA offers twice the titles as PDA—because IPs are being compensated throughout the year and know that one-time purchases are possible.

Why should video producers participate or continue to participate in UDA models? The IPs are concerned about compensation and exposure. They clearly see the value of EBA. With PDA, they understand that their films are being exposed but have concerns about the free uses. We have to maintain a relationship built on trust with our IPs. Many of the pricing models are confusing, so they are trusting us to be honest. We are going to watch over the next year to see how it plays out for all parties involved, so we don't lose anyone's trust. Libraries want everything available through PDA with more free uses, but if IPs are not fairly compensated, they will pull out.

CHAPTER 10

Patron-Driven Acquisition in Public and Special Libraries

IN THIS CHAPTER

- ▷ Examining results of two public library surveys
- ▷ Reviewing a PDA plan for public libraries
- ▷ Summarizing UDA plans in special libraries

PATRON-DRIVEN ACQUISITION (PDA) is the favored term used in the public library field. Although PDA is a relatively new method for most public libraries, this innovative access and purchase model is becoming widely accepted, particularly with consortia. This chapter highlights the results of two surveys: one we conducted in 2015 on PDA in public libraries; and a previously published survey (2012) on e-book use by patrons in public libraries administered by a partnership between the vendor OverDrive and the American Library Association (ALA). The chapter also describes the OverDrive PDA model employed by many public libraries and offers two examples of special libraries that incorporate demand-driven acquisition in their workplace.

PDA Public Library Survey

The goal of our 2015 survey was to canvas public libraries to determine the number and type of PDA plans employed in public libraries (UF Libraries, 2015). The survey was sent to public library listservs, and while the number of responses was relatively low (n = 64), results from the survey provide meaningful analysis of PDA in public libraries. The majority of the survey respondents (59 percent; n = 38) indicated their libraries currently offer a PDA program (UF Libraries, 2015, Q3). Most respondents (81 percent; n = 21) stated the PDA programs were established by their libraries as a "value-added service to patrons" (Q6). An overwhelming percentage of library respondents (88 percent; n =

23) indicated their PDA program was not part of a consortium plan (Q4). Content is selected for the PDA program by librarians (46 percent; n = 12) or by librarians working in combination with vendors (19 percent; n = 5), which indicates that selection is still an important function of librarians (Q5).

The overall impression of the PDA program by most respondents (65 percent; n = 11) is that it complements the collection (Q9). When asked "how do you assess/evaluate the PDA program," the majority of the respondents (59 percent; n = 10) indicated they conduct usage analyses, but only on an annual (24 percent; n = 4) or quarterly (12 percent; n = 2) basis (Q8). Surprisingly, a third (35 percent; n = 6) of the responses stated their libraries do not assess the PDA program.

From the respondents who indicated their library currently does not offer a PDA program, results from a question revealed the reasons for not implementing a PDA program (Q11). The reasons included budget concerns (56 percent; n = 10); technical limitations (28 percent; n = 5); libraries that felt PDA was not an appropriate method for acquisitions in a public library (17 percent; n = 3); and the model was not supported by administrators/board of trustees (11 percent; n = 2). It is worth mentioning that exactly half (50 percent; n = 10) of the survey respondents without a PDA program said they will consider implementing a plan in the future (Q10).

OverDrive and ALA User Survey

In 2012, a large patron survey was conducted by OverDrive in collaboration with the American Library Association's Office for Information Technology Policy that received over seventy-five thousand responses (OverDrive Blogs, 2012). The survey findings would suggest that online borrowing and e-book use is increasing dramatically at public libraries throughout the country (OverDrive and ALA, 2012). Key responses included the following:

- Most of the public library respondents indicated their personal online borrowing of e-books had increased over the past six-month period (60.4 percent; n = 39,267).
- Responses to the question "In a typical month, how often do you visit the library?" show that the average number of visits to the virtual library is 6.9, and 2.4 to the physical library.
- Most patrons download e-books from the public library to e-book readers such as Kindle, Sony Reader, Nook, and so forth (83.5 percent; n = 54,307).
- The majority of responses to the question of "Where did you learn about downloading eBooks for your library?" indicated that patrons "link from the library's website" (52.6 percent; n = 34,208).

What is most telling about these responses is the significant number of public library patrons who visit their "virtual branches" and access and download e-books to readers. Over half of the respondents said they learned about downloading e-books from a link on the library's website, which might suggest not only the excellent method public libraries use to display their online services but also that the e-book navigation to platforms such as OverDrive is made easy for patrons.

The OverDrive PDA Model

A quick online search using the keywords "public libraries" and "mission statement" resulted in two key themes that emerged: to foster lifelong learning, and to build collections to meet the needs of the community by offering a myriad of books, materials, and resources, increasingly online. Public librarians and staff have always responded to patron requests for materials within the scope of tight budgets, so in a sense are "patron driven." Patron-driven acquisition, as described in this book, is a relatively new collection-building initiative in public libraries. Currently there is one major player, OverDrive, which offers a relatively easy-to-use yet innovative PDA model for both libraries and patrons.

OverDrive is a company that offers participating public, corporate, and academic libraries the ability to set up an online digital catalog of e-content (e.g., e-books and audiobooks) that is made readily available to patrons. The OverDrive catalog includes over two million records with e-books, streaming video, and journals/magazines. Libraries in the OverDrive network can purchase items to be offered to their patrons by individual title selection, in preset collections, or both. MARC records for the purchased items are loaded into the library catalog for patron discovery with links to the OverDrive website. Patrons can check out the items using their library cards and download the item to any number of devices including smartphones, tablets, e-book readers (e.g., Kindle), and desktop computers. Circulation policies, such as holds and checkouts in the online environment, are predetermined by the libraries.

A significant number of public and corporate libraries are using OverDrive's PDA model for e-books. If a library has opted in for the PDA model, patrons that discover an e-book or other item on the OverDrive platform not owned by their library will see a message that displays on the screen: "recommend to library" (RTL). A screenshot from the Clevnet Library Cooperation shows how the request for a title displays to the public (see figure 10.1). Users may recommend this title to librarians for purchase (mediated), although in some cases libraries might set up a PDA plan that allows automatic purchase and then access to the titles (unmediated). For mediated requests on the PDA program, there is a wait period for access, but patrons have options to be notified when the book is available or for the book to be automatically checked out to them if and when the item

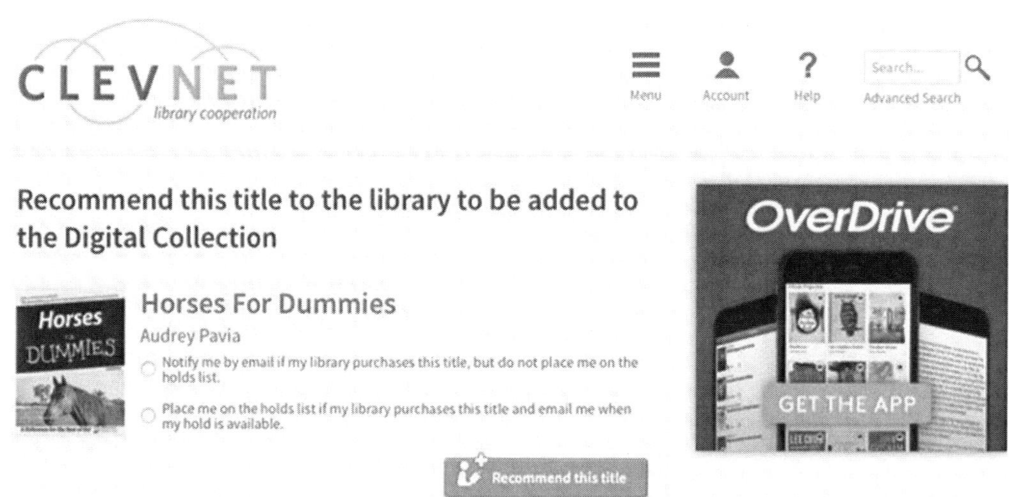

Figure 10.1. Example of a public library catalog record with RTL. Clevnet Library Cooperation.

is purchased. The ease-of-use functionality and features of the OverDrive PDA model drive its success. The presentation and navigation of the OverDrive catalog is similar to the Amazon site, which makes it very user friendly.

At the time of this publication, OverDrive offers a simple but effective PDA model. The entire OverDrive catalog is made available to patrons, so there is no way to place parameters on the content or refine results for what is offered on the PDA program, but there are future plans to do so. Most of the content is a single-user license (i.e., one patron at a time can check out and access the e-book) although libraries can purchase additional copies for popular titles. OverDrive also offers PDA models to academic, special, and corporate libraries. At the time of this publication, OverDrive is the predominant vendor offering PDA to public libraries.

Special Libraries

For the purposes of this book, a special library is a term applied to corporate, medical/health sciences, government, research, or information centers. Use-driven acquisition (UDA) models such as purchase on demand (PoD) are common in special libraries as they offer a varied, patron-driven approach to collection building. Pay per view (PPV) is also a model prominently used by special libraries. PPV is an acquisitions method employed by libraries that allows users to access journal articles at point of need. Libraries partner with publishers/vendors to provide users with online access to individual articles from journals not subscribed to by the library. Instead of subscriptions, libraries pay for the PPV service either through a deposit account or in some cases article by article. It is also similar to many libraries' document delivery service but is much faster, as the users have instantaneous access to the articles.

Medical and Health Libraries

Currently there are a few publishers that offer evidence-based acquisition (EBA) and PDA content for medical and health sciences libraries. Publishers that offer the EBA model provide their content in prepackaged discipline/subject collections, although many times the medical and health science e-books are included in large STEM (science, technology, engineering, and mathematics) and medicine collections. It is relatively easy to find medical and health-related e-books in vendor and aggregator demand-driven acquisition (DDA) plans, as all subject disciplines are made available in this model. Libraries can also create a specific profile to include e-books published only in the medicine and health subject classifications. Of course, libraries can always negotiate with vendors and publishers to work out a more content-specific plan.

Corporate Libraries

Patrons of any for-profit corporate libraries or information centers are internal to the company, and most if not all requests are demand-driven acquisition. For example, when a company solicits bids for a project, competitive intelligence is required. Or in the case of consulting firms, the project manager/consultant requests a literature search from the librarian. The librarian retrieves citations based on the requested parameters, and full-text articles are purchased after the project manager/consultant selects the desired citations.

This model is most efficient for corporate or for-profit libraries (or research centers as they are often named) because, unlike the academic setting, copyright charges and full-text charges apply, which can be quite costly. Furthermore, the vendors and publishers charge significantly more money to corporate libraries for database access. To better understand this workflow, a corporate librarian provides an overview of how she conducts demand-driven acquisitions, more specifically a purchase-on-demand (PoD) plan, to her internal clients. She states,

> Occasionally I buy materials (e.g., books) on a topic, but there is no predetermined budget. When the consultants bid a job, the budget for the cost of literature searches and articles is part of the proposal. I purchase articles from the original website (e.g., Elsevier) and pay the Copyright Clearance Center (CCC) a blanket yearly fee. Articles purchased stay in-house, but the blanket CCC does allow for one copy to the client. The library is legally required to provide the list of citations in EndNote and attach PDFs of the article, and it is only one copy[, which is] not to be distributed [and is] just for certain jobs that require a complete administrative record. It is also important to know the rules and regulations and legal information as well. (Metzger, 2015)

International Libraries

UDA models are not unique to North American libraries. There are many international academic, government, and special libraries (e.g., research centers) that offer some type of UDA model, but this expansive topic is beyond the scope of this book.

In an interview with a librarian who works in an intergovernmental special library in the Philippines, again the issues tend to be budgetary. When asked to describe the type of UDA model in this special library, the librarian states,

> In our case, for books on demand, we need to file a material requisition that is approved by the management. It is quite a slow process, and approval could take a few days up to several weeks. Due to our limited budget for books ($4,000 USD), we buy selected books or prioritize those requested and needed by our researchers. Most of the requested books are sometimes not available from local book dealers or jobbers so we opt for purchasing through Amazon using a credit card. We can save a lot of money by purchasing online and paying for shipping costs. (Alayon, 2015)

As far as articles, this specific library relies heavily on interlibrary loan through various association memberships.

Key Points

PDA models can be applied to public and special libraries and are based on clientele and patrons, copyright laws, and budgets.

- Evidence from the "PDA Public Library Survey" demonstrates that there is an increase of PDA programs offered by public libraries. The type of PDA depends on budget, technical expertise, and administrative support.
- Evidence from the OverDrive and ALA survey shows that patrons have an acceptance of and familiarity with online access and e-book use.
- Special libraries offer a variety of hybrid UDA models.

Next, chapter 11 delves into the evaluation and assessment of UDA plans, including what data to collect, what reports to generate, and how to communicate the results to stakeholders.

References

Alayon, Stephen B. 2015. E-mail to author.

Metzger, Kristen. 2015. Phone interview with author.

OverDrive Blogs. 2012. "Survey Says: Library Borrowers Also Buyers." November 15. http://blogs.overdrive.com/.

OverDrive and ALA (American Library Association). 2012. "Library eBook Survey Hosted by OverDrive and American Library Association (ALA)." http://blogs.overdrive.com/.

University of Florida George A. Smathers Libraries (UF Libraries). 2015. "PDA Public Library Survey." Last updated August 10, 2015. http://ufdcimages.uflib.ufl.edu/IR/00/00/71/93/00001/PDA_Public_Library_Survey.pdf.

Part 4

EVALUATION AND EMERGING STRATEGIES

CHAPTER 11

Assessment of UDA Plans

IN THIS CHAPTER

- ▷ Stating the case for assessment
- ▷ Assessing a UDA Plan
- ▷ Gathering data and creating reports
- ▷ Modifying a plan
- ▷ Communicating results to stakeholders

ASSESSMENT METHODS AND STRATEGIES are critical for building and maintaining an effective use-driven acquisition (UDA) plan. Assessment of the plan should be ongoing, and libraries should be part of the evaluation processes from the start. Techniques for evaluating each UDA model after initial launch are described in previous sections, so this chapter will provide detailed examples that illustrate when and how to run reports to assess a plan throughout its life cycle. Conveying assessment results to the appropriate stakeholders of your library, consortium, or institution is also discussed.

Making the Case for Assessment

There are several reasons for assessment. First, a systematic, well-planned assessment strategy is needed to judge whether the plan is effectively meeting collection and budget goals. The National Information Standards Organization (NISO) demand-driven acquisition (DDA) report stresses the importance of assessment: "It should be an integral part of any DDA program and should be considered early in the planning process," pointing out the two major aspects for assessment are to determine overall effectiveness and predicting expenditures (NISO, 2014). The second reason to conduct assessment is to share

REASONS FOR ASSESSMENT

- ✓ Assessment is necessary to build and maintain an effective UDA plan.
- ✓ The more proactive, not reactive, libraries are in approaching assessment, the more successful the plan will be in the long term.
- ✓ Assessment provides evidence to make modifications that will improve the plan.
- ✓ Assessment provides evidence of cost and usage, and whether these metrics are meeting goals set for the UDA plan.
- ✓ The results of assessment can and should be shared with administration and other library stakeholders, strengthening the library's reputation for data-driven decision making.
- ✓ Once established, an assessment strategy can be implemented that brings value while not being overly labor intensive for the library.
- ✓ Every implementation phase in a UDA plan can be improved by assessment.
- ✓ Assessment for shared and consortia UDA plans is crucial for all the library participants and their stakeholders.

the results of the UDA plan with the stakeholders of the library. Stakeholders can include library directors, collection managers, faculty, researchers, or campus administrators who control the budget. If the assessment proves that the UDA plan is meeting goals and is a valuable acquisitions method, then sharing the reports with stakeholders is the ultimate marketing tool. Whether a library runs reports independently or requests that a book vendor or aggregator handle the bulk of report generation, assessment and evaluation must be an ongoing component of the UDA plan.

Assessment of UDA Plans

It is constructive for libraries to create an assessment strategy before implementing a UDA plan. Libraries should discuss with vendors and publishers early in the negotiation process what reports and data will be offered to the libraries for assessment. In chapter 1, "Use-Driven Acquisition Project Management," a simplified checklist for the basic implementation of a UDA plan includes an entire series of steps for designing an assessment strategy:

Step 1. Determine the data and reports needed.

Step 2. Determine when to evaluate.

Step 3. Check workflow and technical aspects.

Step 4. Track expenditures and usage data.

Step 5. Conduct user studies or surveys.

This section will focus on when to assess the UDA plan, workflow and record loads, cost-and-usage reports, and methods of modifying UDA plans.

Table 11.1. UDA Library Survey, question 11: "How is the PDA/DDA program evaluated?"

#11	ANSWER	RESPONSES	%
1	Run title/cost/usage reports offered at the vendor/publisher site	138	52%
2	Request title/cost/usage reports from vendor/publisher	76	28%
3	Use library-created reports downloaded into Excel or other application	89	33%
4	Other	29	11%
5	Use a hybrid approach between vendor and library	99	37%

Step 1. Determine the Data and Reports Needed

Determining the type of information required from evaluation is the first step in devising a strategy. An assessment strategy should address several aspects of the plan, from the review of workflow to compiling and synthesizing cost-and-usage data. But it is the level of information the library wishes to view or convey that is the key to the next steps in assessment. If a library requires only basic cost-and-usage data, reports issued by publishers or supplied on vendor platforms and databases should suffice. However, to determine whether incoming content is meeting collection goals, or to compile detailed cost-per-use reports, the library will need to develop a more comprehensive assessment strategy and take more responsibility in evaluation.

Based on the "UDA Library Survey," most libraries do not rely entirely on vendors to run reports (see table 11.1). A majority of survey respondents indicate that their libraries generate reports offered at the vendor/publisher websites (52 percent; n = 138), followed by using a hybrid approach for data gathering between the vendor and the library (37 percent; n = 99). Respondents also generate library-created reports that are downloaded into Excel or another application (33 percent; n = 89). A small percentage indicated that they request reports from the vendor/publisher (28 percent; n = 76), and 11 percent do not know how their UDA plan is assessed. Since this question allowed multiple responses, the percentages suggest that libraries are engaged in more than one method of assessing UDA plans, whether independently or in conjunction with vendors and publishers.

Step 2. Determine When to Evaluate

Assessment should be performed more frequently than once or twice a year if results are to be used to make quick adjustments to the plan. Based on responses received from the "UDA Library Survey" regarding the frequency of evaluation, it appears that too many libraries are not running formative assessment plans as often as needed (see table 11.2). Results show that the majority of libraries evaluate their programs annually (43 percent; n = 113), while quite a number evaluate the program biannually (15 percent; n = 40; UF Libraries, 2014, Q12). Fortunately, a large percentage do evaluate their PDA/DDA programs quarterly (33 percent; n = 87). Annual or biannual

Table 11.2. UDA Library Survey, question 12: "How often is your PDA/DDA program evaluated?"

#12	ANSWER	RESPONSES	%
1	Never	24	9%
2	Quarterly	87	33%
3	Biannually	40	15%
4	Annually	113	43%
Total		264	100%

assessments are adequate for gauging the overall effectiveness of a plan or to report back to administrators, but generating monthly or quarterly reports is a more proactive approach and will help sustain a successful program. While it is disappointing that some libraries responded they never evaluate their programs (9 percent; n = 24), it probably indicates these libraries are allowing vendors to generate reports and share their evaluation.

Step 3. Check Workflow and Technical Aspects

After launching a UDA plan, workflow, staffing assignments, and technical elements of the plan should be reviewed immediately and modifications made as necessary. Workflows between vendors, publishers, and libraries should be examined and problems reported as they arise. For evidence-based acquisition (EBA), streaming-video UDA, and other vendor-hosted plans, early assessment is important, but once a plan is up and running, constant attentiveness is usually unnecessary. A library offering publisher and vendor-hosted UDA plans should review the content to ensure it meets the goals and parameters of the plan. A library should also check a subset of the MARC records to ensure links to the platform are functioning properly.

The assessment process for a DDA plan starts with scrutinizing the initial back file (or back run) that vendors provide libraries. This review is the first important step in evaluation, as the back file exemplifies the type and number of e-books that will be offered to library users. Once the initial file of records has been loaded into the library catalog, most of the heavy lifting has been accomplished, although it behooves libraries to monitor the discovery records being added to the catalog in subsequent loads. Libraries should perform a certain amount of quality control on the content, while also keeping an eye on the number of records being loaded going forward. You can expect to see some variance in succeeding record loads, as each file represents the number of e-books issued by the participating publishers that match the profiles of the plan. However, if there is a large increase in the number of records being added in subsequent loads, it can be a flag for concern, as more e-books offered to users usually equates to more usage and higher cost. If a surge in the size of the record loads becomes a pattern, the library should contact the vendor.

Step 4. Track Expenditures and Usage Data

Cost and usage are the principal metrics of any UDA plan. Many libraries have restrictive material budgets, so it is particularly important for a library to track allocation and expenditures for each plan. Usage is also paramount; whether the UDA plan offers e-books, streaming video, journal articles, or print materials, the content has to receive an adequate level of use or it will be discontinued. For a UDA plan to be successful, it must produce a positive cost-usage ratio and deliver a solid return on investment. Usage data showing the number or type of access to content does not necessarily reflect user satisfaction, nor does it reveal the impact the content is having on research or instruction, but data on how much the content is being accessed is extremely important.

Assessment of UDA plans begins with vendor and publisher reports. An example of a publisher's cost-and-usage report for an evidence-based acquisition plan can be seen in table 11.3. The report in Excel includes title, list price, and subject area, plus quarterly and total usage for each e-book. These reports are the basis for selecting what titles to purchase.

Table 11.3. Snapshot of a publisher-supplied cost-usage report for an EBA plan

TITLE	PRICE	SUBJECT	DEC. 2014	JAN. 2015	FEB. 2015	MAR. 2015	TOTAL USES
Biological Materials Science	$195.00	Engineering	15	146	7	34	202
The Economic History of Latin America	$195.00	History; Latin Am.	1	31	33	1	66
An Introduction to the Medieval Bible	$195.00	Religion	0	36	0	0	36
The Long Struggle against Malaria in Tropical Africa	$125.00	History; Africa	0	34	0	0	34
Elements of Logical Reasoning	$195.00	Philosophy	0	25	0	0	25
Arabic	$195.00	Language & linguistics	0	23	0	0	23
Testlet Response Theory and Its Applications	$195.00	Statistics & probability	0	0	0	22	22

For DDA plans, many reports offered by vendors or aggregators are sent or downloaded from vendor websites to library customers in Excel spreadsheets. Typically these reports focus on usage and costs independently, or combine cost with usage but focus on specific actions such as the cost of short-term loans. It is up to the library to sort, compile, and develop tailored cost-and-usage reports independently or in conjunction with vendors. An example of a basic cost-and-usage report as compiled by a library is seen in table 11.4. The spreadsheet report includes the title, publisher, LC class, number of uses,

Table 11.4. Example of a vendor-library cost-usage report for purchased e-books—DDA

USES	TITLE		PUBLISHER	LC CLASS	COST
4	Probability		Wiley	QA	$393.66
3	Words Onscreen		Oxford	Z	$121.38
4	Analyzing and Modeling Spatial & Temporal Dynamics of Infectious Diseases		Wiley	RC	$393.66
3	Plant Life: A Brief History		Oxford	QK	$242.88
6	Meta-Religion		California	BL	$218.70
7	Modeling and Simulation Support . . .		Wiley	TA	$393.66
3	Scripts of Blackness		Illinois	F	$277.02
4	Why Occupy a Square?		Oxford	DT	$60.72
4	Cloud Computing and Electronic Discovery		Wiley	KF	$131.22
11	Brain2Brain		Wiley	RC	$102.06
18	Big Data		Wiley	HD	$63.99
		Total cost-and-use figures			
23,504 uses	1,722 e-books purchased;	$137.16 per title	Cost per use = $10.05		$236,196.81

and the purchase cost for each e-book purchased on the DDA plan. The vendor report was originally sent as a spreadsheet that contained over a dozen fields; most of the fields were then eliminated for this library report. The list was pages long; this example includes library-compiled cost-and-usage totals, with a final cost per use for the entire plan summarized on the bottom page of the report.

Cost and usage can be coupled into a cost-per-use metric, which is often applied in measuring the cost-effectiveness and the return on investment (ROI) of a UDA plan. For an e-book DDA or EBA plan, to determine cost per use, simply divide the purchase cost of an e-book by its total usage. This same formula can be applied for short-term loans (STLs) incurred on a DDA plan; divide the STL costs by the number of loans to determine the cost of each STL. For DDA plans that have purchase and STL costs incurred, you can total all costs and divide by all uses to determine the final cost per use of the plan. If cost per use is determined to be strong, the plan is almost always viewed as a success.

Vendor and aggregator reports made available through their platforms for DDA plans do not always provide librarians with concise cost-and-usage information in one spreadsheet. For in-depth reports that combine cost-and-usage data and summarize cost per use, or to compile and sort the cost and usage into subject areas for drilled-down analysis, libraries will have to request these reports from the vendors, or perform the sorting and compiling themselves. Often the data must be gathered from multiple reports, which requires time and a basic knowledge of programs like Excel or Access.

An example of a library-generated cost-and-usage report for an e-book DDA plan can be seen in table 11.5. This report shows the aggregate number and cost of e-books purchased or accessed by short-term loans during the year. It also includes an average cost per use for e-books purchased or loaned, plus total cost, total usage, and a final average cost per use for the entire DDA plan. This type of report is somewhat labor intensive to create, which is why libraries frequently turn to vendors to generate more elaborate cost-usage reports. While vendors are usually agreeable to such requests, libraries may have to wait days or even weeks to get reports with detailed cost-and-usage information, especially if requested frequently.

An example of a more elaborate cost-and-usage report showing how a library compiled and organized the data received from vendor reports can be seen in table 11.6. This library-generated report provides details from e-books purchased on a UDA plan over a three-year span. The report includes the number of e-book titles purchased, with cost-and-usage figures, subtotaled and divided by Library of Congress (LC) classes to show how various subject disciplines are supported by the DDA plan. The average cost per title is also provided by LC class. The e-book cost-and-usage figures have also been compiled into three broad subject areas—humanities/social sciences, STEM, and medicine—and offer the total number of titles purchased, total cost, and usage for the entire DDA plan. A short report such as this tells a convincing story to collection managers and administrators in a general and concise layout. Whether or not these cost-usage figures met collection and cost-benefit goals for each specific LC class, for the three broad subject areas, or for the entire plan is for the subject specialists and administrators to determine.

Step 5. Conduct User Studies or Surveys

Conducting user studies as they relate to UDA plans is an area that has received little attention. Most users who access e-books received through demand-driven acquisition

Table 11.5. Example of a library-generated cost-use STL report

DDA E-Books Program Report ***Cost-Usage Analysis Performed, April 2014***			
E-books purchased			
Number of e-books purchased		163	
Purchase cost	$24,386.29		
Preliminary cost/e-book purchased			$149.61
STL cost for e-books purchased	$5,498.18		
Total cost of e-books purchased	$29,884.47		
Final cost/e-book purchased			$183.34
STL activity			
Number of STLs for nonpurchased e-books		1,303	
Number of STLs for purchased e-books		326	
STL cost for e-books purchased	$5,498.18		
Remaining cost for STLs only	$19,842.44		
Total cost of STLs	$25,340.62	1,629	
Cost per use (STL)			$15.56
Cost usage of purchased e-books (as of April 2014)			
Total cost		$29,884.47	
Usage		1,657	
Total cost per use of purchased e-books			$18.04
Total cost: usage of purchased and nonpurchased e-books			
Total cost		$49,726.91	
Total usage		3,286	
Total cost per use			$15.13

and evidence-based acquisition plans are unaware their use is driving acquisitions. Print PDAs and purchase-on-demand plans on the other hand offer opportunities to contact users and conduct surveys through checkout of the purchased print materials. This section will not delve into user studies as they pertain to UDA but simply notes its importance as a topic of future research.

Table 11.6. Example of a library-generated cost-usage report for DDA (2009–2012)

COST AND USE OF PURCHASED E-BOOKS BY LC CLASS						
LC CLASS		COST	NUMBER OF TITLES	AVERAGE COST PER TITLE	USAGE	AVERAGE COST PER USE
A	General	$0.00	0	$0.00	0	$0.00
B	Psych; religion	$4,185.78	32	$130.81	522	$8.02
C	Archaeology	$41.78	1	$41.78	4	$10.45
D–F	History	$3,215.96	31	$103.74	363	$8.86
G	Geo; anthro; rec	$2,870.33	20	$143.52	134	$21.42
H–HJ	Econ & business	$6,951.01	67	$103.75	747	$9.31
HM–HX	Sociology	$7,863.65	62	$126.83	1,529	$5.14
J	Political science	$3,400.51	27	$125.94	368	$9.24
L	Education	$2,661.60	23	$115.72	214	$12.44
M	Music	$1,016.00	9	$112.89	263	$3.86
N	Fine arts	$682.69	8	$85.34	71	$9.62
P	Language & lit	$8,820.51	68	$129.71	601	$14.68
TR–Z	Photo; Lib sci	$1,147.53	15	$76.50	155	$7.40
Humanities/social sciences		$42,857.35	363	$118.06	4971	$8.62
Q	Science	$9,475.13	70	$135.36	1,147	$8.26
S	Agriculture	$1,161.07	9	$129.01	78	$14.89
T–TP	Tech/engineering	$5,825.27	44	$132.39	849	$6.86
	STEM	$16,461.47	123	$133.83	2074	$7.94
R	Medicine	$10,076.79	78	$129.19	771	$13.07
All PDA		$69,395.61	564	$123.04	7,816	$8.88

Modifications Based on Assessment

The results from assessment can be applied to modify a UDA plan or to fine-tune a library's collection and budget strategies. For EBA plans, making modifications based on cost and usage is relatively easy. If usage is too low or the cost is too high, a library can elect to forego running an EBA plan or select alternative content.

Demand-driven acquisition plans are another matter altogether, as they require more ongoing assessment compared to the EBA model. The cost of DDA plans often fluctuates, as e-book usage in each library triggers short-term loans and purchases at different rates. Usage and costs are based on the number of records and list price of the e-books in the consideration pool, which will oscillate in size as records are added or removed during the life of the plan. For DDA plans, usage is defined as the number of times an e-book is accessed for a certain period (usually five minutes or more) or where a user activity (such as printing or downloading) triggers a short-term loan or purchase.

Modifying a DDA plan begins with assessing usage and the rate of spend on purchases and short-term loans (if STLs are part of the plan). If the rate of expenditures of the plan is not what the library anticipated, adjustments can be made by raising or lowering price caps for purchases and short-term loans, by removing or adding records by imprint years, or even by including or excluding publishers. All of these modifications can be done with the aim of reducing or increasing content and subsequent expenditures of a DDA plan as needed.

Cost, usage, and other detailed reports can have a larger impact on a library's collection management initiatives and budget allocation. A majority of survey respondents indicated that the results of reports do have an effect on collection-building decisions (UF Libraries, 2014, Q13). For example, if analysis that shows a DDA plan is supplying far more e-book content in the humanities or social sciences and much less in the STEM areas, a library might reallocate funds for e-book EBA plans, firm orders, or package purchases in the science disciplines to balance expenditures and build collections.

Communicating Assessment Results

Everyone likes a good story, but the art of a good story is in the delivery. When reporting on any type of assessment, your goal is to use evidence to tell a story. It is best to avoid supplying too much data, or raw data, and to keep the assessment report simple. The amount and type of data to be included in a report is dependent on the audience and the story you wish to convey. For example, if your audience is library administrators, a cost-benefit report or cost-data summary from the UDA plan is a good strategy. If your audience is outside the library (i.e., campus administrators), the report should be a brief, clear executive summary that avoids library jargon and acronyms.

When writing your assessment story, keep these simple steps in mind: (1) who, (2) what, (3) why, (4) how, and (5) next. Here are a few examples of information to include when communicating with campus administrators, library administrators, and librarians:

- Campus administrators (*who*) want to know the library budget (*what*), such as total expenditures including salaries, collections spending, and so forth. Most importantly, administrators want to know who is using the collection (*why*), type of collection being used, including e-journals, e-books, and databases (*how*), and what is the broader impact. In other words, how is the collection budget increasing productivity of the campus community? It is valuable to include some budgetary figures against peer institutions, but keep in mind that what a library may deem as a peer institution could differ from what your administrator has in mind, so plan to evaluate both. With the peer institution budget evaluations, this is where you can ask for collection budget increases (*next*). This report should be considered an executive summary, not to exceed one page.
- When creating an assessment report for library deans/directors (*who*), include the breakdown of the budget, such as cost of subscriptions, usage, overlap, and costs per discipline, in addition to the information listed above (*what*). It is beneficial to include the scholarly impact of the collections (*why*) and how the collection benefits the mission of the institution. Conclude the report with comparison budget data from perceived peer libraries as justification for additional future funding al-

RECOMMENDATIONS

It is best to keep an assessment report simple so that your audience has the information needed to make informed decisions. When creating and presenting assessment reports on UDA plans, here are some basic elements to consider:

- Be prepared to provide basic definitions and summaries of the UDA models for your audience—especially stakeholders outside the library.
- Be accurate, clear, and concise; the more complex the data, the more simple and clear the message should be.
- Determine how much data is enough to prove your point; do not use raw data.
- Create figures and charts on the UDA plan for your presentation; visual aids are helpful.

locations in addition to identifying new collection trends such as streaming videos (*next*).

- When providing a collections assessment for librarians/selectors/collection managers/bibliographers (*who*), you can summarize the data further to include usage, turnaways, and cost per use, as well as sorting the data by LC classification (*what*). The analysis of the data will be the *why*, and soliciting input for new collection trends and a wish list for purchases should be offered as the *next* section.

Key Points

Although assessment is conducted at various stages of a UDA program, the planning for assessment must be part of the goals and objectives in the initial development of the program. Be prepared for all types of data gathering and reporting for various stakeholders, in and outside the library. Here are some of the most important takeaways:

- Determine the metrics you need to gather when developing an assessment strategy.
- Evaluation reports should be generated to determine if goals are being met, to determine if the plan needs modification, and to convey results to stakeholders.
- Libraries should assess a UDA plan routinely to provide evidence for adjusting profiles, parameters, and costs.
- The review of technical aspects, such as of workflow and discovery files, is a crucial early step in assessment.
- Assessment and reports fuel collection and budget strategies.
- Assessing cost and usage is of prime importance; the cost-per-use metric is key to determining cost-effectiveness.
- For deeper cost-per-use and subject-area analysis, libraries must often sort, compile, and highlight the information into tables and charts that illustrate a message.
- Assessment and reports can garner support from administrators, librarians, and other stakeholders.

The next chapter will summarize trends of the various UDA models and formats discussed in this book.

References

NISO (National Information Standards Organization). 2014. "Demand Driven Acquisition of Monographs: A Recommended Practice of the National Information Standards Organization." June 24. http://www.niso.org/.

University of Florida George A. Smathers Libraries (UF Libraries). 2014. "UDA Library Survey." Last updated August 10, 2015. http://ufdcimages.uflib.ufl.edu/IR/00/00/71/94/00001/UDA_Library_Survey.pdf.

Further Readings

Alan, Robert, Tina E. Chrzastowski, Lisa German, and Lynn Wiley. 2010. "Approval Plan Profile Assessment in Two Large ARL Libraries: University of Illinois at Urbana–Champaign and Pennsylvania State University." *Library Resources and Technical Services* 54, no. 2: 64–76.

Arndt, Theresa S. 2015. *Getting Started with Demand-Driven Acquisitions for E-books: A LITA Guide*. Chicago: ALA TechSource.

Caverly, Sarah H., Amy McColl, Norm Medeiros, and Mike Persick. 2014. "A Hard DDA's Night." In *Customer-Based Collection Development: An Overview*, edited by Karl Bridges, 13–26. Chicago: ALA.

Dewland, Jason C., and Andrew See. 2015. *Library Resources and Technical Services* 59, no. 1: 13–23. http://dx.doi.org/10.5860/lrts.59n1.

Duncan, Cheri Jeanette, and Genya Morgan O'Gara. 2015. "Building Holistic and Agile Collection Development and Assessment." *Performance Measurement and Metrics* 16, no. 1: 62–85. doi:10.1108/PMM-12-2014-0041.

Fleming-May, Rachel, and Jill E. Grogg. 2010. "Chapter 1: Assessing Use and Usage." *Library Technology Reports* 46, no. 6: 5–10.

Griffin, Melanie, Barbara Lewis, and Mark I. Greenberg. 2013. "Data-Driven Decision Making: An Holistic Approach to Assessment in Special Collections Repositories." *Evidence Based Library and Information Practice* 8, no. 2: 225–38.

Huddy, Lorraine. 2012. "Striving for Insights and Contending with Limitations: The Assessment of a Collaborative eBook Project." *Against the Grain* 24, no. 4: 36–40.

Hufford, Jon R. 2013. "A Review of the Literature on Assessment in Academic and Research Libraries, 2005 to August 2011." *Portal: Libraries and the Academy* 13, no. 1: 5–35.

Kelly, Madeline. 2014. "Applying the Tiers of Assessment: A Holistic and Systematic Approach to Assessing Library Collections." *Journal of Academic Librarianship* 40, no. 6: 585–91. doi:10.1016/j.acalib.2014.10.002.

Kyrillidou, Martha, Amy Yeager, and Steve Hiller. 2014. *E-Resource Round Up: 2014 Library Assessment Conference; Building Effective, Sustainable and Practical Assessment*. Vol. 26. doi:10.1080/1941126X.2014.971678.

Martin, Heath, Kimberley Robles-Smith, Julie Garrison, and Doug Way. 2009. "Methods and Strategies for Creating a Culture of Collections Assessment at Comprehensive Universities." *Journal of Electronic Resources Librarianship* 21, no. 3: 213–36. doi:10.1080/19411260903466269.

Mugridge, Rebecca L. 2014. "Technical Services Assessment." *Library Resources and Technical Services* 58, no. 2: 100–110.

Schafer, Mickey. 2013. "Science Communication: Crafting Science Messages." Class lecture, Discovering Research and Communicating Science, University of Florida, Gainesville, September 5.

CHAPTER 12

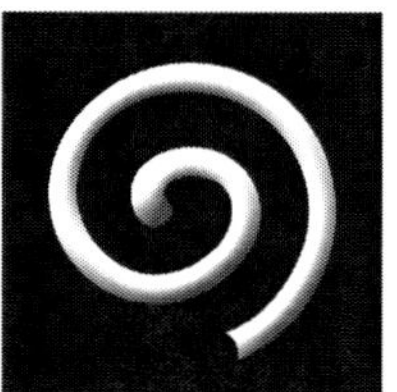

Future Directions

IN THIS CHAPTER

- ▷ Providing foreseeable directions of UDA models
- ▷ Offering recommendations to libraries, vendors, and publishers

THIS CHAPTER PRESENTS A SERIES OF projected future directions and implications for use-driven acquisition (UDA) in the next few years. Each section begins with an overview of the important features of the UDA model or format and then offers potential trends for the future of UDA in libraries. Also included are several recommendations for librarians and content providers to improve the UDA products and services offered to library users.

Directions of UDA

Collections and Budgets

Libraries must first define their collection management objectives to determine the parameters of a UDA plan. While a growing number of libraries are allocating more funds to UDA plans, it is a slow transition. The "UDA Library Survey" reveals that over half of responses indicate their libraries allocate a relatively small percentage (0–10 percent; n = 141) of their materials budgets for UDA plans (UF Libraries, 2014, Q15). Note the following trends:

- More libraries will gradually shift from a *just-in-case* to a *just-in-time* approach to collection building, especially for targeted subject areas.
- Libraries will reallocate larger percentages of their budgets to UDA initiatives.
- Libraries will reallocate materials budgets including routing funds from firm order or approval plans to pay for UDA plans.

- UDA plans will become even more accepted as innovative collection-building tools, and many libraries will revise collection policies accordingly.

Evidence-Based Acquisition (EBA)

EBA offers a variation on traditional demand-driven acquisition plans for e-books and can be an effective complement to aggregator-based DDA plans. Publishers offer EBA plans for e-books, as the predominant format, although some content providers include other formats such as streaming video with this model. EBA allows for the mediation of selection by the libraries, although many times selection is performed based on usage. Note the following trends:

- EBA will become more widespread as the model offers appealing aspects to both libraries and content providers, including little or no DRM restrictions and controlled accounting and regulated spending.
- EBA plans will be built more with profiles instead of prepackaged subject collections. This will allow more flexibility for libraries designing a plan that meets collection goals.

DDA/PDA

E-books are currently the most popular format for UDA plans. A wide majority of respondents (94 percent; n = 274) indicate their libraries are operating a patron-driven acquisition (PDA)/demand-driven acquisition (DDA) e-books plan (UF Libraries, 2014, Q7). Publishers are continuously raising the costs of short-term loans (STLs) resulting in a large impact on the DDA model. Note the following trends:

- E-books will be a more popular format than print books, resulting in an increase of the number of DDA/PDA plans.
- Libraries will take the initiative to make DDA plans more robust. Cost-saving steps may include reducing the purchase triggers; eliminating STLs; excluding publishers who set expensive prices for STLs; and targeting subject areas where publisher content is priced more economically.

Shared and Consortia UDA

Library consortia are leveraging collective buying power due to shrinking budgets and pressures from governing bodies. UDA plans are viewed as a cost-effective method for collaborative collection building. However, many questions are being raised about the sustainability of consortia UDA plans, particularly with DDA. Note the following trends:

- Consortia will continue to implement shared DDA and EBA plans, but new hybrid models will be utilized even more to fill specific needs and budgets of participating libraries.
- Initiatives such as the "rent to own" model, where libraries run a standard DDA plan that includes short-term loan costs rolled into the purchase price of an e-book, will emerge as a compromise for publishers and budget-strapped library groups.

- Consortia will continue to place increased pressure on vendors to develop sustainable, cost-efficient models that are satisfactory to both the libraries and the publishers.
- The future may see libraries align with institutions outside traditional library consortia that better mirror their own goals.

Streaming Video

Streaming-video UDA plans are a new, exciting, and increasingly popular method to acquire films online. Out of all of the formats being incorporated into UDA plans, streaming video has the most potential for growth. Note the following trends:

- Libraries will invest more funding into streaming-video PDA to support course reserves, distance learning, and instructional requirements that are based on actual need.
- Libraries will continue to evaluate the necessity of retaining obsolete and unused formats such as VHS, DVD, and Blu-ray, and instead look to streaming-video EBA and PDA plans as a standard, cost-efficient method of purchasing films.
- Streaming-video content providers will allow more custom collection building for UDA plans in the future, such as à la carte selection or selection based on traditional profiling.

Print Materials PDA

Print materials are still a heavily purchased format for libraries, and while libraries are purchasing more print books than e-books, that gap is narrowing. PDA plans that purchase print books or other print materials (e.g., music scores) from patron requests have an ordering and processing workflow very similar to the purchase-on-demand model. Note the following trends:

- More libraries will test the print PDA model as a pilot plan or establish a new plan, as unused and underused print books are simply unacceptable to many libraries.
- Libraries and vendors will develop new models or improve existing models that offer both print and e-books that allow users a choice of formats.
- More academic libraries will begin to employ print PDA plans for targeted subject areas and traditional print-based collections.

ILL-PoD

Purchase-on-demand (PoD) plans historically acquired a predominant number of print books. PoD is a viable model of acquisitions because the items requested are derived from interlibrary loan (ILL) requests, and research suggests a good portion of the items will receive additional use. Note the following trends:

- PoD plans will become more prevalent in libraries of all types as reduced staffing becomes more of an issue and as ILL borrowing costs continue to rise.
- PoD plans will expand from acquiring mostly print books to include more streaming video, e-books, and other online resources.

- Incorporating print on demand will increase the number of print books purchased directly from user requests at the point of need.

Public and Special Libraries

A growing number of public libraries are launching PDA plans for e-books, journals, videos, and other online resources. Many special libraries use a unique approach to acquiring content using patron-driven acquisition, where online content is purchased on an individual basis and is similar to the PoD model. Note the following trends:

- PDA will become an established and prominent method of offering online content to public library patrons. Libraries will see this method as a way to offer more content to patrons but only purchase items actually requested or accessed.
- PDA vendors will begin to offer more sophisticated profiling and filtering functionality to their PDA plans and allow public libraries more control and ways to target the content offered to patrons.
- Special libraries will offer more articles on demand by utilizing the pay per view (PPV) and PoD models. These models offer a unique method of supplying much-needed content to users that is demand driven and less expensive than purchasing subscriptions.

Vendors and Content Providers

There must be a reciprocal partnership between libraries and vendors/publishers in designing, implementing, and managing UDA plans. Without these collaborative efforts, a UDA plan will not be as effective and probably not sustainable. PDA and DDA plans are challenging to publishers as revenue streams can be affected adversely and are rather unpredictable. Note the following trends:

- Library book vendors experiencing competition from behemoth booksellers such as Amazon will develop new models by adopting a more retail-like atmosphere for discovering and accessing UDA content.
- Content providers will progressively extol the EBA model over the DDA model because EBA often works on a lump-sum-deposit or invoicing schedule and provides more consistent revenue streams.
- Content providers will offer more options for how content is chosen for DDA/PDA plans, allowing libraries more flexibility and the ability to establish plans that reflect their collection goals.

Assessment

Assessment is critical for building and sustaining effective use-driven acquisition (UDA) plans. Libraries must play an active role in evaluating and building reports to monitor crucial metrics as well as applying results to modify UDA plans. It is important for libraries to share reports and the results of a UDA plan with stakeholders. Note the following trends:

- Libraries are spending too much staff time cobbling together usable reports. Content providers and vendors need to develop easy-to-use reports that provide pertinent cost-and-usage data on any UDA plan.

- Libraries will increasingly need to share budget and collections information with stakeholders to demonstrate budgetary prudence and user satisfaction.

Key Points: Recommendations for Publishers, Vendors, and Librarians

Use-driven acquisitions is now an accepted method of acquiring access and purchasing resources for many libraries. A significant number of respondents (89 percent; n = 242) to the "UDA Library Survey" stated they would support the continuation of a PDA/DDA program in their library (UF Libraries, 2014, Q17). UDA is here to stay. In the following section, recommendations are offered to stakeholders involved in UDA plans. Many of these suggestions and observations are often discussed in library literature or at conferences and highlight the importance of the topics for further consideration.

Recommendations for Publishers and Content Providers

- Provide content in the STEM (science, technology, engineering, and mathematics) and medicine subject areas at the same level as the humanities and social sciences (HSS).
- Continue to allow more or all e-books to be multiuser and downloadable across platforms.
- Issue print and e-book versions simultaneously or issue the e-book version first.
- Price the e-book version comparable to the list price of a print book.
- Offer content on shared and consortia e-book plans with reasonable pricing models.
- Allow e-book chapters to be shared at minimal cost via interlibrary loan or allow e-books to be loaned using technology such as Occam's Reader.

Recommendations for Book Vendors and Aggregators

- E-books should be accessible across all of the most common browsers and mobile devices, and in a variety of formats that allow users to select a version compatible with their e-book reader.
- Influence publishers to remove barriers to STEM and medicine content in the PDA models.
- Influence academic publishers to allow the checkout of e-books so users can have access to entire books as is offered to public libraries.
- Convince publishers to issue e-textbooks at a more reasonable cost for libraries.
- Offer enhanced reports, including elaborate cost-usage reports sorted into subject areas that are easy for library staff to generate and distribute.

Recommendations for Librarians

- Course reserves, when possible, should be offered in the electronic versions. Online access is what many users prefer, and it better supports distance-learning initiatives.
- Libraries must provide clear instructions on using e-books on the different platforms and improve communications with users on the parameters set by each publisher or within a platform.

- Libraries, including vendors and publishers, need to improve and standardize e-book catalog records. These records should be at a full level with series and call numbers to improve discoverability.
- Libraries should move beyond the OPAC by migrating to next-generation library systems and discovery platforms; through innovative e-resources and acquisition functionality, these new library systems should improve the management of e-books and UDA plans.
- Libraries should develop clear and efficient ordering, cataloging, and paying workflows for each of the methods of e-book acquisitions.
- Public libraries should request vendors to develop functionality of PDA programs to create profiles and filter the e-book content offered to patrons.
- Libraries need to improve evaluation methods and reports to better communicate their mission and accomplishments to stakeholders.

Reference

University of Florida George A. Smathers Libraries (UF Libraries). 2014. "UDA Library Survey." Last updated August 10, 2015. http://ufdcimages.uflib.ufl.edu/IR/00/00/71/94/00001/UDA_Library_Survey.pdf.

Appendix 1

UDA Library Survey

Answers to the survey questions, including free text responses, are found at the University of Florida's institutional repository ("UDA Library Survey," University of Florida George A. Smathers Libraries, last updated August 10, 2015, http://ufdcimages.uflib.ufl.edu/IR/00/00/71/94/00001/UDA_Library_Survey.pdf).

Thank you for choosing to participate in our survey on patron-driven/demand-driven acquisitions. We appreciate your honest opinion and feedback. The survey is anonymous and will take approximately five minutes.

Q1. In which country/region is your library located?

- United States
- Canada
- Caribbean
- South America
- Europe
- Asia
- Australia
- Africa

Q2. In which type of library are you currently employed?

- Academic (college or university)
- Public
- Special (gov't, museum, research/information center)
- Other ___________________

Q3. What is your primary position in your library?

- library administrator
- library administrator with collection duties
- collection manager/bibliographer/subject specialist

- acquisitions librarian/staff
- other ___________________

Q4. Does your library currently participate in a patron-driven or demand-driven acquisitions (PDA/DDA) program?
- Yes
- No

Q5. Do the following people in your library support the PDA/DDA program?

	YES	NO	NOT SURE
Library Administrators			
Collection Managers/Subject Librarians			
Acquisitions Librarian/Staff			

Q6. What is your impression of the PDA/DDA program in your library? (select all that apply)
- Simple, cost-effective method of acquisitions
- Has its pros and cons
- Inferior method for acquiring specific or appropriate content
- Worried that individual selection/collection manager's role will diminish
- Issues may arise with existing collection methods (e.g., duplication with firm orders)
- Collections become too "trendy" or lopsided
- Other (please explain) ___________________

Q7. What type of PDA/DDA programs are currently operating in your library? (select all that apply)
- E-books
- Print books
- ILL–books on demand/purchase on demand
- Journal articles
- Reference
- Streaming videos
- Consortia
- Course reserves
- Music scores
- Other ___________________

Q8. How do you promote the PDA/DDA program to library patrons? (select all that apply)
- Do not promote the program
- Library newsletter, website, or Twitter
- Promote only to the departments that I support
- Banner on the library homepage

- Message to patrons when their material is purchased through the PDA/DDA program
- Not sure
- Other ____________________

Q9. How are the parameters for content selected for the PDA/DDA program? (select all that apply)
- Used existing approval/slip-plan parameters
- Created new parameters with collection development librarians
- Built your own collection plan
- Vendor developed parameters based on budget and collections
- Library administration created the parameters
- Acquisitions librarian/staff created the parameters
- Not sure

Other ____________________

Q10. How do you manage the number of PDA/DDA records in your catalog? (select all that apply)
- By price limits
- By year of publication (imprint)
- By year available to vendor/publisher
- By using vendor-created add/delete files
- By blocking content from specific publisher
- Not sure
- Other ____________________

Q11. How is the PDA/DDA program evaluated? (select all that apply)
- Run title/cost/usage reports offered at the vendor/publisher site
- Request title/cost/usage reports from vendor/publisher
- Use library-created reports downloaded into Excel or other application
- Use a hybrid approach between vendor and library
- Other ____________________

Q12. How often is your PDA/DDA program evaluated?
- Never
- Quarterly
- Biannually
- Annually

Q13. Do the PDA/DDA reports impact your library collection decision making?
- Yes
- No
- Not sure

Q14. How does your library fund the PDA/DDA program? (select all that apply)
- From funding in addition to the collection budget (e.g., endowments)
- From firm or approval book funds
- From a discretionary fund approved by library administrators

- Not sure
- Other ___________________

Q15. Approximately what percentage of your library materials budget is allocated for PDA/DDA plans?
- Not relevant
- 0–10 percent
- 11–20 percent
- 21–50 percent
- Over 50 percent
- Not sure

Q16. How satisfied are you with your PDA/DDA program in your library?
- Very dissatisfied
- Dissatisfied
- Somewhat dissatisfied
- Neutral
- Somewhat satisfied
- Satisfied
- Very satisfied

Q17. Would you support the continuation of a PDA/DDA program in your library?
- Yes
- No
- Not sure

Q18. Will your library add a PDA/DDA pilot or program in the future?
- Yes
- No
- Not sure

Q19. What are the reasons that your library does not currently incorporate a PDA/DDA program in your library? (select all that apply)
- Library budget constraints
- Not supported by library administrators
- Not supported by collection managers/subject specialists
- Does not fit well with our existing collection development policy
- Not relevant to our patrons' needs
- Limited staff available to manage a PDA/DDA program
- Uncertain that a PDA/DDA program is an appropriate method of acquisitions
- Would like to implement a PDA/DDA program but not sure how to start one up
- Other ___________________

Appendix 2
PDA Public Library Survey

Answers to the survey questions, including free text responses, are found at the University of Florida's institutional repository ("PDA Public Library Survey," University of Florida George A. Smathers Libraries, last updated August 10, 2015, http://ufdcimages.uflib.ufl.edu/IR/00/00/71/93/00001/PDA_Public_Library_Survey.pdf).

Thank you for choosing to participate in our survey on patron-driven acquisition (PDA) programs in public libraries. We appreciate your honest opinion and feedback. The survey is anonymous and will take approximately five minutes. Please click the ">>" button below to continue.

Q1. Select the type of public library where you are currently employed:
- Association (1)
- Municipal, county (2)
- Municipal, city (3)
- Municipal, town (4)
- Municipal, village (5)
- School district (6)
- Special district (7)
- Other (8) ____________________

Q2. What is your position at the library? (Please select your primary role)
- Administrator/manager/supervisor (1)
- Librarian (2)
- Library staff (3)
- Volunteer (4)
- Other (5) ____________________

Q3. Does your library currently offer a patron-driven acquisition (PDA) program?
- Yes (1)
- No (2)

Q4. Is your PDA program part of a consortium?
- Yes (1)
- No (2)

Q5. How do you select the content for the PDA program?
- Librarians choose the scope of the content. (1)
- All-inclusive collections offered by the vendor (2)
- Combination of library and vendor (3)
- I don't know (4)
- Other (5) ____________________

Q6. Why did you establish a PDA program at your library?
- Administration decision (1)
- Value-added service to patrons (2)
- Part of a consortia agreement with other public libraries (3)
- I don't know (4)

Q7. Approximately what percentage of your current annual budget is allocated for the PDA program?
- ______ 0–100 percent (1)

Q8. How do you assess/evaluate the PDA program? (Select all that apply)
- By usage statistics, including number of downloads (1)
- By cost of the PDA program (2)
- On an annual basis (3)
- On a biannual basis (4)
- Quarterly (5)
- Patron satisfaction survey (6)
- We do not currently assess/evaluate (7)
- I don't know (8)

Q9. What is your overall impression of the PDA program? (Select all that apply)
- Patrons love it! (1)
- Complements the collection (2)
- Has its pros and cons (3)
- Simple, cost-effective method for buying e-books (4)
- Other (5) ____________________

Q10. Will you consider implementing a PDA program in the future?
- Yes (1)
- No (2)
- I don't know (3)

Q11. What are the reasons for not implementing a PDA program? (Select all that apply)
- Budget (1)
- Library administrators/board of trustees are not supportive. (2)
- Technical limitations (3)

- PDA programs are not an appropriate method of acquisitions for a public library. (4)
- Other (5) ____________________

Q12. Based on your understanding, what are your overall impressions of patron-driven acquisition programs? (Select all that apply)

- I wish we had a PDA program at our library. (1)
- Patrons request/recommend this type of service to be added. (2)
- Not an appropriate method for building a library collection (3)
- Other (4) ____________________

Glossary

access versus ownership. Phrase used to describe opposing views of collection building in libraries. Libraries often face the dilemma of which is more important: providing access to content or owning that content in perpetuity.

aggregator. A vendor that provides access to content from multiple publishers through a single platform or interface. Examples include EBSCO, Ebrary, and EBL.

approval plan. Method of collection development in which print and e-books that match a predetermined set of parameters (*see* profile) are automatically routed to the library from a book vendor but can be returned if deemed unsuitable.

blanket order. Similar to an approval plan, a method of collection building in which a library commits to the ongoing, bulk purchase of books and other materials made available from a content provider based on established parameters targeting specific subject areas.

COUNTER reports. Counting Online Usage of Networked Electronic Resources. These are standards that dictate the collection and reporting of usage reports and allow librarians to track usage consistently across electronic content providers.

DDA. Demand-driven acquisition. Also known as "PDA" or "patron-driven acquisition." Method of collection development in which content is not loaned or purchased unless it is actually used.

discovery pool. Often called "consideration pool." Set of titles made available to library users that have not yet been purchased.

discovery service. Form of search engine used by libraries to provide users with a single tool for searching and retrieving results from multiple databases and resources. Examples include Summon, Primo, and EBSCO Discovery Service.

DRM. Digital rights management. Technological measures employed by content providers to limit the amount of electronic content that can be printed, downloaded, copied, and so forth, by the user.

e-book platforms. The interfaces employed by publishers and aggregators through which users read and manipulate e-books.

EBA. Evidence-based acquisition. Also called "EBS," or "evidence-based selection." Method of collection development that allows library users access to online content for a set period of time. Once that time is up, librarians make purchasing decisions based on evidence of use.

firm order. Common method of collection development in which individual titles are purchased at the library's discretion.

hybrid plans. Acquisition plans that include various elements of PDA/DDA and even EBA models; the plans often incorporate both print and e-books, and may merge traditional methods of acquisition as well.

interlibrary loan (ILL). This service typically has three functions: borrowing and lending of materials, and document delivery of articles electronically. ILL traditionally focused on print book sharing, but document delivery is increasing and vital for many libraries.

***just in case* versus *just in time*.** Integral predicament facing libraries that raises the question of whether to purchase content just in case it may be used, or to only purchase content at the point of need. Many libraries strive for a balance between the two.

MARC (machine-readable cataloguing) records. Bibliographic records containing coded fields of information such as title, author, and subject heading that are loaded into a library's catalog and/or discovery service for users to access. Most UDA plans use vendor or publisher-supplied MARC records for e-books and other resources.

mediated purchase. Content is only purchased through manual librarian intervention.

PDA. *See* DDA.

pilot program. An experiment with preset time limits that allows a library to test new initiatives within a controlled environment before committing to a large-scale project.

profile. Set of subject and nonsubject parameters created through a library/vendor partnership that controls the scope of content supplied to the library. Profiles can work for a variety of collection development methods, including DDA/PDA and EBA plans.

slip notifications. Method of collection development in which notifications of new titles are sent to libraries, allowing librarians to make title-by-title purchasing decisions.

STL. Short-term loan. Method of access in which the publisher or vendor provides limited-time access to an e-book for a percentage of the price of that e-book. Libraries set preferred loan periods and can negotiate with content providers to determine the number of loans that can be accrued before the e-book is purchased.

turnaway. Occurs when a certain threshold of users accessing a single title at the same time is reached.

UDA. Use-driven acquisition. Umbrella term used to describe any method of collection development in which content is loaned, purchased, or accessed based on actual need instead of anticipated need.

unmediated purchase. Content is purchased automatically without librarian intervention.

vendor. A commercial content provider that partners with multiple publishers and aggregators to deliver access to print and electronic content. Vendors offer value-added services such as cataloging and processing, MARC records, and profiles.

Index

aggregators, 26, *75*, 155
  list of, *28*
  recommendations for, 146
API. *See* application program interface
application program interface (API), 88
assessment, 30, 31, 131–41
  communicating results, 139, 140
  examples of reports, *115*, *135*, *137*, *138*
  future directions of, 145, 146
  modifications based on, 138, 139
  reasons for, *132*
  UDA plans, 132–37

back file title list. *See* backrun
back run, 47–48

collection planning, 13–15
  future directions of, 142
consideration pool. *See* discovery pool
consortia:
  budgeting, 73
  consortia plans, 70–77
  DDA models of, 73, 74
  EBA plans, 62–63
  future directions of, 143, 144
  interlibrary loan, 102
  phases of implementation, *72*
  reasons to launch, *71*
  working with vendors and publishers, 74–76
corporate libraries, 125, 126. *See also* public and special libraries
COUNTER reports/usage statistics, 30, 49, 63, 64, 113, 155

DDA. *See* demand-driven acquisition
demand-driven acquisition (DDA), 39–57, 155
  de-duplication of e-books, 48
  definition of, 4
  e-books, 39–51
  evaluation, 49
  future directions of, 143
  licensing models, *41*
  pilot program, 42, 43
  profile creation, 42–47
  profile revision, 47, 48
  project planning, 50
  rate of spend, 42–*43*
  selection models, *40*–42
digital rights management (DRM), 26, 155
discovery pool, 28, 45, 155
DRM. *See* digital rights management

EBA. *See* evidence-based acquisition
evidence-based acquisition (EBA), 26, 58–69, 155
  assessment, 63, 64
  budgeting, 60, 61
  content providers, *60*
  de-duplication, 62
  definition of, 4
  future directions of, 143
  selection models, 59, 60
  streaming video, 109–10

Interlibrary Loan–Purchase on Demand (ILL-PoD), 95–107, 156
  assessment, 101, 102
  case studies, 104–7
  consortia, 102
  definition of, 4
  evaluation of, 101, 102
  future directions of, 144, 145
  pilot program, 97, 98, 99
  reasons to implement, *96*
international libraries, 126. *See also* public and special libraries

Library of Congress classification, 45

MARC records, 29, 48, 62, 88, 90, 112, 156
marketing, 112,13
medical and health libraries, 125. *See also* public and special libraries

National Library of Medicine classification, 45

patron-driven acquisition (PDA):
  definition of, 4
  evaluation of, 90, 91
  future directions of, 143, 144
  implementation of print plans, 86, 87
  print materials, 85–91
  in public and special libraries, 122–30 (*see also* public and special libraries)
  profile creation for print books, 87
  streaming videos, 110
  workflows for print books, 88–90
PDA. *See* patron-driven acquisition
pay per view (PPV):
  budgeting, 18
  definition of, 4
  in special libraries, 125, 145
print materials. *See also* patron-driven acquisition
public and special libraries, 122–27
  corporate, 125, 126
  future directions of, 145
  international, 126
  medical and health, 125
  OverDrive model, 124, 125
  surveys of, 122, 123, 152–54
publishers, 26, 46
  list of, *28*
  recommendations for, 146
purchase-on-demand. *See* Interlibrary Load-Purchase on Demand (ILL-PoD)

shared plans. *See* consortia
short-term loans (STL), 41, 42, 156
STL. *See* short-term loans
streaming video, 108–21
  case study, 116–18
  evaluation of, 113–15
  evidence-based acquisition, 109, 110
  future directions of, 144
  models, 109, 110
  patron-driven acquisition, 110
  reasons to implement, 109
  vendors, 109

UDA. *See* use-driven acquisitions
use-driven acquisitions:
  approval plans, 16, 17, 155
  budgeting, 17–19, 142, 143
  definition of, xiii, xiv, 156
  future directions of, 142–47
  overview, 3, 4
  pilot program, 9
  project management, 5–8
  reasons to implement, *14*
  survey of, 148–51

vendors, 25–36, *75*, 109, 156
  choosing, 25, 26
  collaborating with, 76
  evaluation of, 30, 31
  future directions of, 145
  list of, *28*
  recommendations for, 146
  responsibilities, *32*
  training, 29, 30

About the Authors and Contributor

Steven Carrico has a B.A. in art history and a master's in library information science from the University of Illinois. Steven has been an acquisitions librarian at the University of Florida Smathers Libraries for more than twenty years and is currently chair of the Acquisitions Department and collections coordinator. His research includes use-driven acquisitions, collection and materials budget management, e-book use, and collection-user assessment in academic and special libraries.

Michelle Leonard, an associate university librarian in the Marston Science Library (part of the University of Florida Libraries), holds an M.A. and master's in library science from Kent State University, Ohio. She serves as the collection subject specialist for entomology and nematology, environmental sciences, geological sciences, the School of Natural Resources and Environment, and wildlife ecology and conservation. Michelle implemented the libraries' first "books-on-demand" pilot program in 2006 when she managed interlibrary loan and course reserves services, where books are purchased based on requests from the UF faculty and graduate students. She has published several papers in peer-reviewed journals and has received invitations to speak at conferences on the national level and international level about collection metrics, purchase on demand (PoD), and use-driven acquisition (UDA) plans.

Erin Gallagher has a B.A. in English and a master's in library and information science from Florida State University. After working for a book vendor as a collections consultant, she delved back into academic libraries with a particular focus on electronic resources management, use-driven collection development, and vendor-library relations. She is currently the e-resources and serials librarian at Rollins College in Winter Park, Florida.

Trey Shelton has a B.A. in retail merchandising from the University of Montevallo and a master's in library and information science from the University of South Florida. Trey began his academic library career managing monograph and serial acquisitions at the University of Florida and currently serves as the e-resources librarian. His research focuses primarily on cost, use, and usage studies as related to data-driven decision making, acquisitions and e-resources workflow analysis and best practices, and collection development. Trey regularly presents at conferences and has published several articles and conference proceedings papers.